P9-ARV-536

THE
LIFE OF PHILIDOR

Da Capo Press Music Reprint Series
GENERAL EDITOR
FREDERICK FREEDMAN
VASSAR COLLEGE

THE
LIFE OF PHILIDOR

MUSICIAN AND CHESS-PLAYER

By George Allen

Supplementary Essay by
Tassilo von Heydebrand und der Lasa

S DA CAPO PRESS • NEW YORK • 1971

A Da Capo Press Reprint Edition

This Da Capo Press edition of
The Life of Philidor
is an unabridged republication of the first
American edition published in Philadelphia
in 1863.

Library of Congress Catalog Card Number 70-139198

SBN 306-70075-1

Published by Da Capo Press
A Division of Plenum Publishing Corporation
227 West 17th Street, New York, N.Y. 10011

LIFE OF PHILIDOR

BY

GEORGE ALLEN

THE

LIFE OF PHILIDOR

MUSICIAN AND CHESS-PLAYER

BY

GEORGE ALLEN

Greek Profeffor in the Univerfity of Pennfylvania

WITH A SUPPLEMENTARY ESSAY ON

PHILIDOR

AS CHESS-AUTHOR AND CHESS-PLAYER

BY

TASSILO VON HEYDEBRAND UND DER LASA

Envoy Extraordinary and Minifter Plenipotentiary of the King of
Pruffia at the Court of Saxe-Weimar

PHILADELPHIA

E. H. BUTLER & CO.

LONDON C. J. SKEET   *PARIS* G. BOSSANGE & Cɪᴇ
LEIPZIG ERNST SCHÄFER

1863

PHILADELPHIA:

CAXTON PRESS OF C. SHERMAN, SON & CO.

PREFACE.

THE ſpecial and indiſpenſable original ſources of information for the life of Philidor are the following:—I. A biographical notice in the work of his pupil, La Borde (*Eſſai ſur la Muſique*, 4 vols. 4to. Paris 1760.) This notice was baſed on memoranda furniſhed by Philidor himſelf, rather over fifteen years before his death; but it brings his *perſonal* hiſtory down no lower than 1754, the date of his return from England.—II. The "*Anecdotes of Mr. Philidor, communicated by himſelf*" in *Cheſs* [by Richard Twiſs, F.R.S.] vol. i. 1787, pp. 149–71, with the additional anecdotes in *Cheſs*, vol. ii. 1789, pp. 215–18, and the "*Cloſure of the account of Mr. Philidor*," in Twiſs's *Miſcellanies*, 1805, vol. ii. pp. 105–14. Theſe anecdotes, while they confirm the notice of La Borde, are far more copious, and conſtitute the chief reliance of the biographer.—III. The article *Philidor peint par lui-même*, in the ſeventh volume of Saint-Amant's *Palamède*, (pp. 2–16,) compoſed by J. Lardin from matter prepared by Philidor's eldeſt ſon, André, who ſurvived until 1845. It embraces a biographical notice, which the ſon had completed, and a number of random anecdotes. The notice contains little beyond what appears to have been derived from Twiſs's *Cheſs*;

but the anecdotes, worthlefs as a portion of them may be, are of peculiar intereft and value, for the light which they throw upon Philidor's perfonal charaĉter and habits.—IV. A fpecimen of the letters which Philidor was in the habit of writing home, during his annual vifits to London. Thefe important documents are found in the *Palamède* for 1847, pp. 172–8.

Now many Lives of Philidor have been written, in the fhape of articles in works of general and fpecial Biography; but they differ fingularly from each other, in reference to the ufe made in them of the above-defcribed original authorities. Of courfe, none but fuch as have been written fince 1847 could exhibit anything derived from the matter furnifhed in Saint-Amant's *Palamède*. But of the others—and they are nearly all— it is a curious faĉt, that none but fuch as have been written by Chefs-authors (and I might even fay by *Englifh* Chefs-authors) have fhewn any knowledge whatever of the *Anecdotes* of Twifs. Hence Mr. George Walker's very agreeable *Biographical Sketch* (prefixed to his edition of the *Analyfis*, in 1832) and the appropriate chapter in Mr. Tomlinfon's delightful *Amufements in Chefs*, both bafed upon Twifs, are by far the beft of all that appeared before André Philidor's pofthumous notice. As to *French* Chefs-authors, all they have of Twifs has been obtained at fecond hand: the flight and inaccurate *Biographie*, for example, in the firft volume of La Bourdonnais's *Palamède*—the produĉtion, moft likely, of the lazy and carelefs "King of the Chefs-board" himfelf—is made up from the *Biographical Sketch* of Mr. Walker; and the brief notice in the Comte de Bafterot's moft attraĉtive *Nouveau Traité élémentaire* appears to be bafed direĉtly upon the correfponding chapter in the *Amufements* of Mr. Tomlinfon.

As for the numerous lives ot Philidor, written by

other than Chefs-authors—articles in Encyclopædias,
Biographical Dictionaries, and Dictionaries of Mufical
Hiftory and Biography—thefe, whether French or Englifh, are, for the moft part, mere tracings after the fketch
of La Borde, with only fo much of unauthentic anecdote
or goffip, as each writer might happen to pick up from
cafual fources of information. Of thefe, that which was
contributed to the *Biographie, Univerfelle* of the Brothers
Michaud, by Sévelinges, is not merely defective, like the
reft, but pofitively mifchievous: it contains that calum-
nious charge of plagiarifm, which has been regularly
copied by the fecond-rate compilers, who have ftolen
their materials from that vaft quarry. The very able
article on Philidor, in M. Fétis's *Biographie Univerfelle
des Muficiens,* for its fingular merits and its very original
defects, ftands entirely by itfelf. It is unique in the
value of its criticifm of Philidor's mufical works—made,
as it was, after careful ftudy of the engraved fcores, now
fo little known and fo difficult to procure; and it is
triumphant in its vindication of the probity, as well as
of the genius, of Philidor. On the other hand, it is
equally unique as a piece of perfonal biography. Fétis
knew nothing of Twifs, and he wrote before André
Philidor. Although a Chefs-player himfelf, and a frequenter of the *Café de la Régence,* he appears never to
have read, or to have treated with contempt, the *Biographie* of La Bourdonnais's *Palamède.* Nothing was left
him, therefore, but La Borde; and La Borde he regarded
with a fcorn fo intolerant and fo abfolute, that he would
not accept as fatisfactory even thofe particulars of Philidor's foreign refidence, which at the fame moment he
tells us were contributed by Philidor himfelf. Nay,
when he finds the German, Gerber, repeating thofe
fame particulars, and fubftantiating them by independent
teftimony, he as little fcruples to fmother Gerber, as to
throw overboard La Borde. To fupply the lack of per-

fonal details, of which he thus robs himfelf, he is forced
to fill up his fketch with La Régence goffip; and this,
where it is, in its way, injurious to Philidor, has been
unfortunately and unfufpectingly copied by the mufical
writers, who naturally defer to the high authority of
Fétis—fuch as Adam, Scudo, and Pougin.

From that which I have thus, with all freedom, faid
of my predeceffors, it may be fufficiently inferred, what
I have myfelf aimed to make the Life of Philidor now
prefented to the Reader. It might, perhaps, have been
more what it fhould be, if it had not been originally,
like its fellows, a mere *article*—the fruit, too, of accidental authorfhip in the field of my recreations, rather
than in that of my profeffional ftudies. The truth is,
that, having fucceeded in collecting a remarkable Chefs-
library—now one of the five or fix in exiftence, that approach completenefs—I was induced, in 1857–8, more
readily than I could have fuppofed poffible, to contribute
to the *American Chefs Monthly*, (which had then juft
been eftablifhed by the able bibliographer and philolo-
gift, Mr. DANIEL W. FISKE,) a feries of articles on the
perfonal biography of Philidor, of which fifty copies
were feparately printed for private diftribution. The
reception of my biography, in either form, by the Chefs-
world, to which alone it was then addreffed, was fo unexpectedly favourable,* that, when my illuftrious correfpondent, Herr VON DER LASA, offered to contribute a
fupplementary paper on *Philidor as Chefs-author and*

---

* The celebrated French Chefs-*littérateurs*, MM. DOAZAN and ST.-
ELME LE DUC, in particular, made a moft graceful recognition of what
I had endeavoured to do for the memory of their great countryman,
by publicly infcribing to me—the former his charmingly written mo-
nographs entitled *La Bourdonnais-Morphy* and *M. Alliey*, the latter a
beautiful article in *La Régence* on his precious Ceylon Chefs-board;
and the learned German Mafter, Herr MAX LANGE, did me the honour to prefent a free verfion of my Biography to his countrymen,
(with praife far beyond its deferts,) in the *Schachzeitung*.

Chefs-player, I decided at once—quite contrary to my
original intention—to give the work a careful revifion,
and to publifh it in the ordinary mode.

To be perfectly frank, however, I muft own, that my
decifion was not a little affected alfo by the temptation.
to indulge certain philobiblian taftes of mine, long fuppreffed but profoundly inveterate. Laying to my foul
the flattering unction, that better Grecians than I had
been bitten with the *Bibliomania*—that Brunck, for example, (who was a gentleman and a foldier, before he was
a fcholar,) never put forth one of his editions without
having copies printed on Large Paper and at leaft one for
himfelf on Vellum—I accepted it as a good reafon for
publifhing my own trifling volume, that I fhould thereby
have the opportunity of "inaugurating" book-printing
on Vellum in America.* The fuppofed difficulty of the
undertaking gave it the charm of an adventure. From
Dibdin—with whofe pages I had often dallied too fond-
ly—I had learned, that the Englifh experiments of his
day, although made by a Bulmer, had been decided fail-
ures, the caufe of which lay (as he believed) in the bad
quality of the imported material. With entire confidence in the fkill of our Philadelphia preffmen, I was
equally fure, that the relations of my friends, Meffrs.
John Penington & Son, to the honourable houfe of
Hector Bossange & Cie at Paris would fecure me the beft
vellum to be had anywhere. Nor was I difappointed.
M. Bossange Senior—ever ready to oblige his American

---

* In mercy to future Panzers and Van Praets, I will reconcile be-
forehand fome apparent conflict of dates by ftating precifely, that after
the work had been carried on into the laft fheet of the Life proper in
1859, it was fufpended; and that, before it was refumed, (viz., in the
fpring of 1860,) two copies of another little book of mine (the *No-
vena to St. Antony of Padua,* pp. viii and 1–24,) were printed on Vellum in the fame Office; while Mr. George Livermore, of Bofton,
had three Vellum-copies of the *Souldiers Pocket Bible* (pp. viii and
1–16) executed by Mr. Houghton, of the Riverfide Prefs, Cambridge.

clientèle—not only caufed the fkins to be examined and
feleted by an *expert*, but alfo forwarded me, from the
fame fource, full and minute inftruions for the guidance
of the preffman—the want of which was the *real* caufe,
I fufpect, of the failure of Bulmer. With fuch ample
preparations and precautions, the work has been executed with entire fuccefs.

I have only to ftate, in conclufion, that I have been
induced, by the confideration that but few take any intereft in Bibliography, to detach from the Life of Philidor
the original Appendix on the editions of the *Analyfe.*
This *Bibliotheca Philidoriana* will, however, be fpeedily
printed by itfelf, with many correions and additions.

G. A.

Philadelphia, June 13th, 1863.

[*Prefixed to the private edition of* 1858.]

TO

DANIEL WILLARD FISKE, Esq.,

EDITOR OF THE CHESS MONTHLY.

MY DEAR FISKE,

To no one, with fo much propriety as to you, could this poor attempt at Chefs-biography, in its prefent form, be infcribed, for it has been yours from the beginning. You led the way to it, by your own beautiful lives of Guftavus Selenus and of Domenico Ponziani. It was written *for* you—to relieve you from fome portion of your editorial labours, during your abforbing engagements with that Firft American Chefs-Congrefs, whereof you were, at every ftage, fo large a part. And when I appealed to the good-nature of our common friend, Mr. Miller, to allow me the troublefome favour of a feparate impreffion, what I had chiefly in view was the opportunity, by dedicating it to you, of expreffing how highly I eftimated the value of your fervices in the caufe of American Chefs and of American Chefs-literature. I muft add, however, that as the work began to reach its conclufion, an additional motive for fuch colleftive impreffion began to force itfelf upon my mind. I reflefted,

that there ſtill remained many unpubliſhed letters of Philidor—that there ſtill ſurvived many recollections and
traditions, by which ſome of his opinions, ſome of the
events of his life, and the circumſtances of his ſolitary
death and burial might be cleared up ; and I ventured to
indulge the hope, that the private diſtribution of my
papers, in a collected form, among ſome of the Cheſs-
literati of France and England, might operate as a direct
appeal to them to ſecure the publication of ſuch additional materials before it ſhould yet be too late.   Even
if diſappointed in this hope, I ſhall not regret having
joined you, my dear Fiſke, in the attempt to record the
perſonal hiſtory of the Cheſs-heroes of other lands and
of other times.   The work is at leaſt a pious one ; and, as
ſuch, may be deſtined, perhaps, to an appropriate reward :—ſome foreign author, of a happier inſpiration
than mine, may one day ariſe to embalm the career of
our Cheſs-hero in a record as laſting, as that which has
preſerved forever the memory of Lionardo da Cutri and
Paolo Boi of Syracuſe.   The diſtant adventure, upon
which the youthful PAUL MORPHY has gone forth, is
not leſs chivalrous, than thoſe which won for that earlier IL PUTTINO the title of the *Cheſs Knight-errant* :—
may he too find his Aleſſandro Salvio ; and thus, by a
double title, ſhine to poſterity not the leaſt brilliant among
the " LIGHTS AND SPLENDOURS OF THE GAME OF CHESS !"

I remain, MY DEAR FISKE,

Your friend and coadjutor,

GEO. ALLEN.

PHILADELPHIA, Auguſt 2d, 1858.

LIFE OF PHILIDOR.

CHAPTER I.

EARLY YEARS—MUSIC AND CHESS.

N the early part of the feventeenth century, an Italian hautboy-player, from Sienna, by the name of *Filidori*, vifited France, and produced a ftrong impreffion on the mind of Louis XIII. by his brilliant performance. Meanwhile a young fubject of the King's, Michel Danican* by name, had been ftudying the fame inftrument, in his native Dauphiné, with fuch fuccefs, that his fkill went far beyond

---

* If the royalift general, Augufte Danican, was really (as Quérard affirms) of the fame ftock as Philidor, (even if not his fon,) and if the new *Biographie Générale* be correct in faying that the General was of a decayed *noble* family, then either a *nom de fief* may have been dropt, or the actual name may have been fpelt originally with the ariftocratic *de*, viz., *D'Anican*.

anything until then known in France.   He, too,
came to Paris, a few years after the vifit of the admired Italian; and when he had been admitted to
play before the Court, his powerful inftrument fo
ftirred up in the foul of the King the recollection
of his "fweeteft of muficians," that he exclaimed—
"*I have recovered my Filidori . . . I have found a fecond
Philidor!*"   The *fobriquet* of PHILIDOR, beftowed
under circumftances fo impreffive, remained ever
after infeparably attached to Michel Danican and
his numerous fucceffors.   He himfelf was immediately made mufician of the royal Chapel; his fon,
of the fame name, (born in 1635,) was likewife
hautboy-player, both in the Chapel and in the King's
private band; and the race of Philidors, always
multiplying and always clinging to the profeffion of
their Dauphinais progenitor, (for one even beat the
kettle-drum, for lack of talent to compafs any higher
attainment,)* had, by and by, come to form a large
element in the compofition of the King's mufical
eftablifhment.†

The third‡ Michel Danican, after having long

---

* "Le fecond était Tymbalier des Menus-plaifirs, n'ayant jamais
pu parvenir à faire autre chose." *La Borde.*

† The facts given by La Borde and Twifs have here received fome
flight addition and interpretation from Fétis.

‡ La Borde, Twifs, André Philidor, and Lardin all agree in making
Philidor's father to have been the *fecond,* and not the *third,* Michel—

filled the poſt of baſſoon-player to Louis XIV., was
permitted by Louis XV., in 1724, to retire on a penſion. He fixed himſelf at Dreux, near Paris ; and
there FRANÇOIS-ANDRÉ DANICAN-PHILIDOR was
born, on the 7th day of September, 1726.* He was
the firſt ſon by a third wife,—a woman (ſays her
deſcendant) of a character ſingularly unſophiſticated
and ſimple. Theſe qualities were reproduced in her
ſon, in a proportion as remarkable as his ſhare in the
muſical endowment of his race.† At the age of

---

to have been the *ſon*, and not the *grandſon*, of the Dauphinais hautboy-
player. I believe them all to be in the wrong, and that Fétis (whom
I follow) is in the right, partly becauſe he appears to have conſulted
authentic documents, and partly for other reaſons, which will preſently
appear.

  * Here Fétis gives the date of 1727, upon the authority of the
valuable MSS. of Beffara, (*Biographie des Muſiciens*, art. BEFFARA.)
But M. Fétis appears to have ſeen the engraved portrait by Bartolozzi,
and might have reflected, that the date attached to it was moſt probably given upon the authority of Philidor himſelf; and *we* have (what
Fétis had not) not only the teſtimony of Twiſs's Anecdotes, but alſo
the legal certificate, (*acte de naiſſance*,) which Lardin profeſſes to have
had in his hands.

  † The other biographers make her a ſecond wife. I follow Lardin,
who alſo (as a proof, perhaps, of her extreme ſimplicity) makes her at
nineteen marry a huſband of ſeventy-three. He gives our hero, at his
birth, a ſiſter of fifty-ſix years old; and will have him to be one of
eight children, born between 1726 and 1730, when his father died—a
period of only four years. Such an account, although coming from a
deſcendant, is clearly not to be relied upon. According to Fétis, Philidor's father, Michel the third, was but fifty at the time of his laſt

fix, after the death of his father, André was admitted one of the Pages of the royal Chapel, at Verfailles, and was thus put, for his mufical education, under the veteran Campra, who was both *Maître de Chapelle* and alfo, by fpecial patent, Teacher of the Pages. This admiffion was four years earlier than the age prefcribed by the rules of the Chapel. The favour was, therefore, probably due to the influence of his numerous relations in the King's fervice, and to the fupport which their reprefentations derived from evidences of his extraordinary precocity of mufical talent, and of his docility of difpofition. His boyifh treble could be made available at once; and his literary ftudies* were probably made to keep even pace with his exercifes in Harmony and Counterpoint. The rigid old Campra was not at all the

marriage. The other biographers, as we have feen, affume his father to have been the fecond Michel; and this, probably, is the fecret of the bridegroom's advanced age.

* Nothing is faid, in my authorities, of Philidor's literary education; but I affume it to have been received under Campra's fuperintendence, becaufe I underftand, (from Grétry's *Mémoires* and other fources,) that the *Maitrifes* (or refidences of the *Maitres de Mufique*) of Cathedrals— and *à fortiori* of a Chapel Royal—were complete *Schools*, in which (as in the *Confervatories* of Italy) the pupils were lodged and ftrictly looked after, while they were carefully taught, along with their profeffion, whatever was neceffarily affociated with it. Some knowledge of *Latin* —the language of the Church fervices, which formed the ufual theme of compofition—appears, therefore, to have formed part of Philidor's education as a Page.

man to fpoil a pupil by letting him grafp too foon at
the reputation of being a mufical prodigy. When,
therefore, he allowed a Motett, with grand chorufes
—the compofition of the boy-page, at the age of
eleven years—to be performed in the royal Chapel,
before the King himfelf, he gave the ftrongeft poffible teftimony to the genius of Philidor, to his remarkable precocity, and to the thoroughnefs of his
early attainments in mufical fcience. The King
encouraged the talent and rewarded the proficiency
of the young Page—who feems to have won everybody's love and efteem from boyhood upwards—
by kindly complimenting him and adding a prefent
of five *louis.** The boy perfevered in his ftudies,
and wrote four Motetts more. At length, when
he had completed his mufical education, and when
the age of fourteen had put an end to his pagefhip,
he left the royal Chapel, and began to fupport
himfelf in Paris by copying mufic, and by giving
leffons to a few pupils. "This (fays Twifs) was in
1740, when feveral *Motetts* of his compofition were

---

* It is Fétis who informs us of the ten-year rule. He, therefore,
will not admit that Philidor became a Page until 1737. Campra
would not, he fays, allow a boy to produce a Motett, when he had
been ftudying only one year. This is no doubt true. But M. Fétis,
inftead of inferring, that Philidor might poffibly have been admitted
earlier than ftrict rule allowed, prefers to infer that the Motett was never
written. André Philidor makes the Motett to have been written at
twelve, and the King's prefent to have been ten *louis.*

performed at Paris at the *Concert Spirituel*, which were favourably received by the public as the productions of a child, who was already a Mafter and Teacher of Mufic."

But the profeffional activity of young Philidor began now to be interfered with by that fafcinating purfuit, which he was never willing to acknowledge as anything for him but a fecondary object at beft, but to which he owes his permanent reputation. He had already learned Chefs while attached to the royal Chapel. The Kings of France, in thofe days, heard Mafs with mufic every morning. The time during which eighty muficians waited, near the Sanctuary, for the King's approach and the beginning of Mafs, muft have hung heavily enough upon their hands; and fome means of amufement were confiderately allowed them. Cards were forbidden; but a long table, inlaid with fix Chefs-boards, was provided—by the higher intellects (we muft prefume) of the mufical corps. It was in fuch facred proximities, from muficians waiting to accompany with voice and inftrument the Holy Sacrifice, that Philidor learned Chefs.*   When he left the Chapel

---

* So much, and no more, fay La Borde and Twifs. But André Philidor tells us the following ftory: "Philidor had often looked over the board with attention, but without ever playing himfelf, when, one morning, an old mufician, who had come to his poft rather early, grumbled a little at having nobody there to play his game of Chefs

he had the reputation of being the beſt player in the band; and he may have flattered himſelf, that this reputation was worth ſomething, ſo long as he frequented only ſuch of the numerous *Cafés,* wherein

---

with. The boy, with modeſt heſitation, offered himſelf to do what he could. Such an offer, from a boy under ten, ſeemed ridiculous enough, but was merrily accepted. As the game went on, the laughter changed to wonder, and the wonder to wrath. The boy watched the darkening of the cloud, and accompanied the approach of checkmate with ſuch a gradual ſliding along towards the end of the bench, that when the ſtorm burſt he was able to reach the door too ſoon for the old limbs of the 'enraged muſician.' The next day there was a ſcramble for the honour of playing with the 'marvellous boy.'" I believe this ſtory to be true, in ſpite of my fixed diſtruſt of André's accuracy, becauſe it is perfeɕtly true to nature—true to the talent and curioſity of the gifted boy, and true to the poſition of deferential inferiority, in which lads of ten were kept, before *La jeune France* and *Young America* had come into faſhion. It is, beſides, preciſely what occurred in the caſe of my venerable colleague, Profeſſor Vethake, the Provoſt of our Univerſity. Mr. Vethake's father, while playing daily with a neighbor, had obſerved that his ſon, then only nine years old, ſeemed to look over the board with ſingular attention. He, therefore, ſaid to him, one day, "Henry, you appear to take great intereſt in Cheſs—I think I muſt teach you the game." "But, Papa, I know the game already." "Why, who has taught you?" "Nobody; I have learnt it by ſeeing you play." "Sit down, then, and try a game with me." The boy took his place at the board to play his firſt game, and filial piety did not prevent him from beating his father ſoundly. His ſecond game—or a very early one, at any rate—was played againſt a learned and ſkilful, but choleric, Dutch gentleman, who anſwered the boy's *Checkmate,* by knocking him down with the board. Of Profeſſor Vethake's later career as a Cheſs-player I have ſaid ſomething in a Letter on *Cheſs in Philadelphia,* contributed to the *Book of the Congreſs.*

Chefs was played, as have left no name behind.
But, by and by, his good fortune guided his fteps to
the immortal CAFÉ DE LA RÉGENCE, and feated him
oppofite to quite another player than had graced any
of the fix facred boards. M. de Kermur, Sire de
Légal,* at that time about forty years old, reigned
fupreme in that famous *Café*, and was undoubtedly a player of extraordinary ftrength; for Philidor
alone was ever able to beat him, and that, too, not
until he had developed his entire force by playing
with Sir Abraham Janffen and the Syrian Stamma.†
The "firft player of the band" found it neceffary to
accept the Rook from M. de Légal; and it took
full three years to work his way up, through the
various degrees of odds, to the honour of confronting
his mafter, on even terms, as a "firft-rate."‡

---

* This great player's name is varioufly written *Kermur, Sire de
Legalle*, by Twifs, and *Kermur* and *Kermuy, Sire de Légal*, by others.
In the Lift of Subfcribers to Philidor's fecond edition it ftands as in
Twifs, but the fpelling was, probably, in both cafes Philidor's own.
The account of Légal, given in the *London Magazine* for May, 1825,
I take to be one of thofe fictions, under the garb of hiftory, which
have infefted Chefs-literature ftill more vexatioufly fince the days of the
wretched La Bourdonnais and Méry *Palamède*.   Diderot calls him "le
profond," and adds, "on peut être homme d'efprit et grand joueur
d'échecs, comme Légal." (St. Amant's *Palamède*, t. ii. p. 88.)

† Fétis fays that old Chefs-players at the *Café de la Régence* had
repeated to him Philidor's own ftatement, that he did not attain his
full ftrength until he had made his campaigns in Holland and in England.

‡ Philidor's communications to Twifs fhow that he received odds,

At this ſtage of his progreſs, the power of playing blindfold was diſcovered to exiſt in Philidor; and in the utter ignorance, on everybody's part, of what had been done in that way by the Paladins of the great Italian School, a hundred and fifty years before, the ſenſation excited by the young prodigy's feats was like that with which Paganini electrified the world, in the days of my "fair and ſhining youth."* M. de Légal, it ſeems, had once tried, when young, to play a ſingle game blindfold, but found himſelf ſo abſolutely exhauſted that he never repeated the experiment.† It now occurred to him, to aſk Philidor, one day, "Whether he had ever tried to play from

---

for three years, from his maſter, but they do not ſpecify the gradation. That he received the Rook at firſt is an old *La Régence* tradition, and is probably true. La Bourdonnais uſed to take the Rook from Captain Harry Wilſon, a player certainly far inferior to Légal. Deſchapelles alone, if we are willing to be of the few or none that believe his famous ſtory, roſe to the rank of a firſt-rate, in twenty-four hours, without ever receiving odds of any kind.

* [Or like that, (I may now add,) which has been made, in the ſociety of London and Paris, during the laſt ſeaſon, by the *eight* ſimultaneous blindfold games of PAUL MORPHY.]

† See Diderot's account of his converſation with Légal (then nearly eighty years old) in reference to Philidor's blindfold exhibitions in London, (St. Amant's *Palamède,* t. vii. p. 180.) I cite the words of Diderot's letter (April 10, 1782). "Au reſte, j'en ai parlé a Monſieur de Légal; et voici ſa réponſe: 'Quand j'étais jeune je m'aviſai de jouer une ſeule partie d'Echecs ſans avoir les yeux ſur le Damier; et à la fin de cette partie, je me trouvai la tête ſi fatiguée, que ce fut la première et la dernière fois de ma vie.' "

memory, without feeing the board? Philidor replied, that as he had calculated moves, and even
whole games, at night in bed, he thought he could
do it, and immediately played a game with the Abbé
Chenard, which he won without feeing the board,
and without hefitating upon any of the moves.—
Philidor then finding he could readily play a fingle
game, offered to play two games at the fame time,
which he did at a Coffee-houfe."*   Such an exhi-

---

* Twifs (*Chefs*, vol. i. p. 151.)—Twifs merely gives the queftion by
Légal: I have endeavoured to account for that queftion by connecting
it with the ftatement made by Légal to Diderot.   La Bourdonnais (or
whoever was the author of the trifling *Biographie* in the firft volume
of his *Palamède*) ftates the matter thus: "There was a converfation
going on, one day, (he fays,) in the prefence of M. de Légal and
Philidor in reference to the great Italian players.   Some were mentioned, who had played feveral games at a time, blindfold.   M. de
Légal appeared not only to doubt the reality of the alleged facts, but
alfo to think the thing impoffible.   Philidor replied, that he could not
agree with him; that he had often recalled difficult pofitions, in the
night, etc." (*Palamède*, t. i. p. 149.)   There is both fiction and mif-
chief in this.   To difguife La Bourdonnais's failure in the attempt to
equal Philidor in. blindfold playing, Philidor's achievements were mif-
reprefented and depreciated in La Bourdonnais and Méry's *Palamède*.
In this paffage of the *Biographie*, the object was to make it appear,
that Philidor knew, at the outfet, that the great Italians, Paclo Boi
and the Jefuit Saccheri, had been wont to play four blindfold games at
once; that he was, therefore, neither unique nor original (as he was
fuppofed to be) in the poffeffion of this faculty; and that in playing
three games at once, with the knowledge of a higher ftandard, he had
undoubtedly reached the utmoft limit of his powers.   Méry even hints,
in another place, (*Palamède*, t. ii. pp. 6–7,) that Philidor's *real* limit

bition of fancy and memory was too novel and too portentous not to have been often repeated; it was a phenomenon for the pſychologiſt no leſs than for the Cheſs-player; and the celebrity of the hero was extended far beyond the limits of the royal Chapel and of the *Café de la Régence.* At that period, Diderot and D'Alembert were meditating their too famous *Encyclopédie,* and when, a few years later, they began to iſſue volume after volume, they did not forget, although Philidor himſelf was living abroad at the time, to record the pſychological phe-

---

was the ſame as La Bourdonnais's, viz., *two* games at once—a piece of miſrepreſentation for which he was juſtly cenſured by M. St. Amant in his *Palamède,* (t. vii. pp. 179, 180.) Now, the alleged diſbelief of Légal in the poſſibility of blindfold playing is inconſiſtent with his own ſtatement to Diderot, that he had played one ſuch game himſelf. The converſation, therefore, could never have taken place; it is "an invention of the enemy." For my own part, I do not believe that Philidor ever attained the full development of his powers in either mode of playing. If he had really been aware, that Paolo Boi had played four ſimultaneous games, I think that Philidor, when in the fulneſs of youthful ſtrength and health, could and would have done the ſame—juſt as we have ſeen Mr. Harrwitz play eight games after Paul Morphy. That Philidor and everybody elſe, at that day, were as ignorant of Cheſs-Literature as I have ſaid, is alſo affirmed by the unfriendly authority of Vogt, (*Letters,* pp. 86–87.) The alluſions of Philidor to Carrera, in the Preface to the firſt edition of his *Analyſe,* are ſo expreſſed, as to prove, that he had not read what he ſtrangely calls "this big book on *the origin and progreſs* of the game;" but had merely got from it—what did not abſolutely require a knowledge of Italian—a proper name or two, with a *Game* or a *Poſition.*

nomenon, of which they had undoubtedly been witneffes.*

It is obvious enough, that a light-hearted youth
of from fourteen to eighteen could hardly be expected to fit all day ftudying Chefs with Légal, at
the *Café de la Régence*—to be enjoying the fenfation created by his blindfold games—and at the fame
time to keep regular hours with his mufic pupils.
He neglected them, (as he admitted to Twifs), and
they confequently took another mafter. It muft
not be inferred, however, that the neglect of his
pupils amounted to an abandonment of his profeffion.
He would never, probably, have been a punctual
Teacher, at any rate—Chefs or no Chefs—and that
becaufe he had, with the genius, the temperament of a
Compofer:—he was always abfolutely abforbed by his
mufical meditations, no lefs than, at another hour,

---

* I copy the language of the *Encyclopédie* from Twifs: " We had
at Paris, a young man of eighteen, who played at the fame time two
games at Chefs, without feeing the boards, beating two antagonifts, to
either of whom he, though a firft-rate player, could only give the advantage of a Knight, when feeing the board. We fhall add to this
account, a circumftance of which we were eye-witneffes : In the middle
of one of his games, a falfe move was defignedly made, which after a
great number of moves he difcovered, and placed the piece where it
ought to have been at firft. This young man is named Mr. Philidor,
the fon of a mufician of repute ; he himfelf is a great mufician, and,
perhaps, the beft player of Polifh Draughts there ever was, or ever will
be. This is among the moft extraordinary examples of ftrength of
memory, and imagination."

by his game; and he was as little capable of taking
note of time in one cafe as in the other. But if we
accept his too honeft confeffion, that Chefs fpoiled
him for a Teacher, in his youth, let us be fair
enough to accept, with equal readinefs of affent, his
later declaration, that Mufic had at no time ceafed
to be his ftudy.* Such a declaration, after the event,
may always, indeed, be, in the nature of things, a
little fufpicious; but that of Philidor happens to be
fupported—for this period, at leaft—by abundant
proof. During his moft affiduous practice of Chefs,
with M. de Légal, Philidor regularly carried his annual tribute of a Motett to the royal Chapel, at
Verfailles; when the Chevalier de Jaucourt recorded
his feats of blindfold playing, he faid—not that he
had been—but that he *was*, at the time, a "great
mufician;" and the firft of that feries of journeys,
by which his reputation as a Chefs-player was
fpread over Europe, was undertaken folely in pur-
fuance of a mufical engagement. Nay, it is as a
mufician, doing profeffional work by contract, that
Philidor figures in a tranfaction of this very period—
a tranfaction, which exhibits him in clofe relations
with the Philofopher of Geneva.

---

* In the advertifement, which Philidor inferted in the *Public Ad-
vertifer*, December 9th, 1753, he affirmed "that the Art of Mufic
had been at all times his conftant ftudy and application, and Chefs only
his diverfion."—Twifs, (*Chefs*, vol. ii. p. 216.)

Jean-Jacques Rouffeau had come to Paris, in 1741, at the age of twenty-nine, with the expectation of gaining a name and fortune by means of a new fcheme of mufical notation. Failing in this, and reafoning, that he might fecure the fame ends by proving himfelf to be *firft* in fomething elfe, juft as well, he began daily to frequent the *Café de la Régence*, and to contend with its ftrongeft players for the primacy of Chefs.* He was beaten by them all; but he played refolutely on, with the affured conviction, that he fhould, one day, have his turn of beating them. He chofe his adverfaries wifely—for among them he names both Philidor and Légal. Before he had fucceeded in beating either of them, he was called away to Venice, to take the place of private fecretary to the French ambaffador. On his return to Paris, in 1745, he returned alfo to his old opinion, that he was to achieve greatnefs by means of Mufic. To that end, he refumed a work, which he had laid afide, when entering on his Chefs-campaign—an Opera, namely, in three acts, entitled *Les Mufes galantes*. This he wifhed to bring out, at firft, privately, at the houfe of M. de la Popeli-nière, who, as *fermier-général*, was a genuine fuc-ceffor of the munificent *furintendant*, Nicolas Fou-quet. Like Fouquet, La Popelinière was fond of

---

* The hiftory of Rouffeau's learning Chefs, a few years before, is given by him in an amufing paragraph of his *Confeffions*, (liv. v.)

feeing himfelf furrounded by men of mind and mark, with little regard to birth, or ftanding, or even to character; and his manfion, at Paffy, was made to contain every appliance for enabling the artifts, who fought his patronage, to exhibit their talents under the moft favourable aufpices. He had his Theatre, with Marmontel for his dramatic poet. He had his Chapel, too; and his Organift and *Maître de Cha-pelle* was no other than Rameau.*

It may be taken as a matter of courfe, that young Philidor, in his double character of precocious Mu-fician and portentous Chefs-player, had been preffed into what was called La Popelinière's *ménagerie*, nor could any formal *procès-verbal*, duly authenticated, add ftrength to my affurance, that Philidor's Motetts took their turn in La Popelinière's Chapel, under the direction of his friend Rameau, and that Philidor's exhibition of blindfold playing had been repeated in La Popelinière's drawing-room, before a company, which embraced the Duc de Richelieu and Diderot, the painter La Tour, and the unrivalled mechanift, Vaucanfon, fide by fide with every fort of foreign virtuofo and adventurer. Philidor was, at any rate, the common friend of many of the celebrities, that formed this affemblage; and when the compofer of *Les Mufes galantes* required the help of a thorough-

---

* What I fay of M. de la Popelinière is derived from a very in-terefting article in the *Biographie Univerfelle.*

bred mufician to lick his really genial production into a prefentable fhape, it was to young Philidor that he applied.

To what extent, and with what fuccefs, Philidor affifted Rouffeau, is ftated differently by different parties. There feems to have been a tradition in Philidor's family, that he executed his tafk with characteriftic abnegation of felf—that he fo managed his fymphonies and accompaniments, as to keep them entirely fubordinate, while they gave relief to the melodies of the amateur compofer.* But, from Rouffeau's own account, on the other hand, it would at leaft appear, that any efforts Philidor may have made to preferve the appearance of unity in the workmanfhip had been entirely unfuccefsful. Rameau praifed the Overture, indeed,—but not as being the production of Rouffeau; and to the execution of the Opera itfelf he liftened with various indications, now of impatience and now of fufpicion, until at laft he exclaimed—ill-naturedly enough—that part of what he had heard was the work of a confummate mufician, and the reft that of the mereft ignoramus in the art. Honeft Jean-Jacques, therefore, is not at

---

* Such is Lardin's ftatement in the *Palamède*, t. vii. p. 11, only that he fpeaks of Philidor's affiftance as given to Rouffeau for *Le Devin du Village*. But this was impoffible : *Le Devin du Village* was compofed and reprefented two years before Philidor's return from his nine years' refidence abroad.

all difpofed to overftate what had been contributed
to the aforefaid "ignoramus" by the "confummate
mufician." He makes Philidor to have done but
little; nor does he give the leaft hint, that that little
was what drew forth the praife of Rameau.* Without attempting to decide between the compofer and
his critic, it is enough for my prefent purpofe to have
fhown, by an incident of fome intereft in itfelf, that
down to the laft of Philidor's early days in Paris,
before his long refidence abroad, he had never
ceafed to be a Mufician, in the practice of his art.

---

* *Confeffions,* liv. vii.

CHAPTER II.

PHILIDOR'S RESIDENCE ABROAD.

 OWARDS the clofe of the fame year, 1745, in which Philidor had been lending his profeffional affiftance to Jean-Jacques Rouffeau, he was induced to leave home, for a fhort mufical tour, which was unexpectedly converted into a long refidence abroad.* At his age, and in his fituation, the tour—even if its accidental refult had been forefeen—could have prefented itfelf to his mind

* If, as Twifs informs us, Philidor went to Holland in 1745, and—about a twelvemonth later—to England in 1747, he muft have left home quite near the clofe of the year 1745. This inference is ftrengthened by the confideration, that his affiftance to Rouffeau appears to have been given immediately before the rehearfal at La Popelinière's, in the prefence of the Duc de Richelieu. But Richelieu was an aide-de-camp of Louis XV. during the campaign of that fummer, and could hardly have returned to Paris before the King, viz., on the 7th of September. The rehearfal was probably ftill later than that date; for Rouffeau did not begin to work on his Opera until long after his return from Venice in the fpring—the fummer having been devoted to Thérèfe Levaffeur—and he was not a rapid worker.

only as a moſt attractive adventure. He was now
barely nineteen, and—although mature in profeſſional knowledge, and by no means frivolous or
irregular in character and habits—was full of youthful ſpirits and enterprise. Hardly a year, moreover,
had elapſed, ſince he had begun to attract attention,
in Pariſian circles, as a phenomenon; and the proſ-
pect of appearing in the ſame character, among the
curious, the learned, and the noble, in foreign coun-
tries, would naturally be a moſt agreeable one.
He had no pupils, and no official connexion with
either Theatre or Chapel, to bind him to Paris.
Nay, as a muſician of genius, born to be a reformer
of his country's muſic, he muſt have already begun
to feel ſome vague longing, at leaſt, to ſeek elſe-
where for ſomething that ſhould better meet the
ideal, now gradually ſhaping itſelf in his mind, than
what he was daily familiar with, and to ſatiety, at
home. Under theſe circumſtances, even a leſs in-
viting opening than that which actually preſented
itſelf, might have been a ſufficient inducement to
young Philidor to "try his fortune," for a time,
among ſtrangers.*

---

* I ſaid before, (p. 13,) that Philidor went abroad ſolely in purſu-
ance of a muſical engagement. Such appears to have been the only
reaſon given by him to Twiſs. But La Borde muſt have heard from
Philidor the other ſide of the caſe: he ſays, that Philidor's progreſs in
Cheſs excited in him the deſire of travelling, to "try his luck" (*pour*

A new phenomenon appeared, about that time, at
Paris, in the perfon of a young harpfichord-player
of thirteen, the daughter of an Italian by the name
of LANZA.   Such a *virtuofa* was fo regular a fubject for "Sultan" La Popelinière's *ménagerie*, that
the imagination waits for no other evidence, to picture her as exhibiting her fkill in the manfion at

---

tenter fortune).   Gerber, author of the *Hiftorifch-Biographifches Lexicon
der Tonkünftler*, (Leipfic, 1792,) although he knew nothing of Twifs,
and bafed his article on La Borde, had the good fenfe, neverthelefs, to
interpret La Borde by his own knowledge of Philidor's occupations in
Germany.   He therefore fays: "The progrefs, which he had, by this
means, made in his art, and efpecially the fkill, which he had at the
fame time acquired in Chefs, excited in him the defire to try his fortune in foreign lands." (2. Theil, 127.)   Undoubtedly, a mufical engagement furnifhed Philidor the *occafion* for going abroad : he had other
motives, however, befides the defire of profeffional improvement, for
being glad that fuch an occafion fhould have prefented itfelf; but I do
by no means recognife, as even *one* of thofe motives—what M. Fétis
makes the *only* one—the wifh or the neceffity of *abfconding* to get rid
of debts.   To believe, that a boy of nineteen could have been in fuch
a fituation, we muft have fome reafonable fhow of evidence.   But M.
Fétis's fole authority was "a celebrated Chefs-player," one M. Dunant,
who did not know enough of Philidor to know where he was, from
1745 to 1754.   And yet this idle ftory is repeated—with the gratuitous
improvement, that creditors were the ftanding torment of his life (*la
grande plaie de fa vie*)—by a very clever author of the day, who—
while meaning well by Philidor—has been fo far from going behind
his carelefs authorities, as to follow them in relating that Philidor,
like Handel, became blind—fuch being the French verfion of "playing without fight of board and men." (P. Scudo, *Critique et Littérature
Muficales*, deuxième férie, pp. 472–3.)

Paſſy, with the bright-eyed François-André, among the reſt, for an admiring liſtener. At all events, Philidor became acquainted with the father. Signor Lanza, it appears—whether juſt arrived from England, or not—had made an arrangement with the celebrated violiniſt, Geminiani, who was then reſiding at London, to meet him in Holland, for the purpoſe of giving twelve ſubſcription-concerts, in which the young harpſichord-wonder was to perform. He now engaged Philidor to be of the party and of the adventure. As Philidor never played on any inſtrument—the kettle-drum of his anceſtor being as much beyond his ſkill as the baſſoon of his father —his part in the concerts muſt have been one, in which either his ſcience was called into requiſition, or ſuch vocal powers as his pageſhip had left him. At the moment of ſetting out on the journey, the daughter was indiſpoſed. She was, therefore, left behind, with her mother, at Paris, until ſhe ſhould be able to travel; while the father proceeded to Holland, in company with Philidor, to keep his appointment with Geminiani. At Rotterdam, where the party (it would ſeem) was to rendezvous, there arrived—not the daughter of Signor Lanza—but the news of her death. The whole concert-ſcheme, with all its proſpects of emolument, was thus ſuddenly deſtroyed by the hand of fate; and our ſanguine adventurer, whoſe reſources had been entirely profpective, now found himfelf pennilefs and a ftranger in a foreign city.

The deftitution and involuntary exile, which had fo fuddenly and violently come on "as an armed man," muft certainly, at firft, have given a fevere fhock to the fpirits of the young mufician, whofe boyhood and youth, up to that day, had bafked in the funfhine of affection and of the admiration due to his double inheritance of genius. But Philidor was too amiably attractive to be left long without friends anywhere, and too cheerful by organization ever to defpair. He had, undoubtedly, already learned, while awaiting the arrival of the poor *Signorina*, that if Rotterdam could boaft of no claffic *Café de la Régence*, with its order of Chefs-magnates, it could point to plenty of homely coffeehoufes, where pairs of heavy Dutchmen fat pondering over a larger board; deliberately puzzling their brains with the intricacies of Polifh Draughts. Philidor's remarkable fkill in this difficult and fcientific game may have been rated too high in the *Encyclopédie*, it contributed little to his celebrity, and he himfelf took no great pride in it; but it now did him yeoman's fervice.*   He became at once a Maf-

---

* "Philidor's fkill in Polifh Draughts is rather overrated by the writers of this article, [in the *Encyclopédie*,] as we know that, although a firft-rate, he was not equal to M. Le Blonde, and feveral other great players of that day. In a voluminous collection of critical ends of games at Polifh Draughts, (publifhed by Dufour, Paris, 1808,) I find

ter among the Dutch Draught-players; and upon
what he earned in this capacity, whether in the
fhape of fees or of ftakes, he lived for a time—and,
apparently, in no diftrefs—firft, at Rotterdam, and
afterwards at Amfterdam.*

But the political capital of the country, now that
a winter of cabinet-councils and diplomatic confer-
ences had fucceeded to an eventful campaign,
prefented greater attractions to Philidor, than the
coffee-houfes of the great commercial cities. He
proceeded, therefore, to the Hague; and there he
remained during the greater part of his refidence in
Holland. It was not, however, the cunning men
of peace alone, that he found there. The armies
had gone into winter-quarters; and many of the
officers were now, of courfe, at liberty to exchange

---

fix ingenious pofitions of Philidor's compofition." (Walker's *Biogra-*
phical Sketch, p. xiv. note.) A correfpondent of the La Bourdonnais
Palamède (tome iv. p. 120) fpeaks, on the other hand, of Philidor as
"le premier joueur de Dames connu." St. Amant (*Palamède*, tome
vii. p. 15, note) probably means to go no farther than Walker: "Il
était également aux Dames d'une force tout-à-fait fupérieure, mais n'y
attachait pas le même amour-propre qu'aux Échecs."

* The following memorandum of Twifs (vol. i. p. 3) points to a
later refidence of Philidor's at Rotterdam: "Mr. Philidor informed
me that he faw, in 1747, at Rotterdam, in the poffeffion of a coffee-
houfe keeper, a fet of Chefs-men, which were made for Prince Eugene.
They were three inches in height, of folid filver, chafed; not different
in colour, but fufficiently diftinguifhed, by one fide reprefenting an
European, and the other an Afiatic, army."

the monotony of mere camp-duty for the gay life of
a city thronged with foreign vifitors.   Among them
fome were found as ready to fhow their prowefs in
mimic as in real war ; and at the gentle Frenchman's
Chefs-board there doubtlefs came to fit, in peaceful
meditation, many a furvivor of that array of warriors, who, on the 11th of May, before, had ftrug-
gled, with indomitable hardihood, in fublime advance and ftill fublimer retreat, to "keep front and
rear together," in the memorable column of Fontenoy.*   The chivalrous Sir John Ligonier, who had
acted as the royal Duke's military tutor on that
bloody day, had been recalled to England, to head
Gardiner's dragoons—fo long as they would face
the Highland hoft—at Falkirk ; but he had left behind him his relative, Colonel la Deves ; and to him
Philidor gave the Knight in many a Chefs-encounter.
The Prince of Waldeck, who had feen his Dutch
divifion behave fo ill at Fontenoy, had met with ftill
another difafter at Rocoux.   He, too, was at the
Hague, ready to receive a Piece from the youthful

---

* Should military hiftories fail to preferve the memory of this battle, it will ftill be remembered, for it has been lightened upon by the
genius of Scott.   Who can read without a thrill Edie Ochiltree's
queftion : "Francie Magraw, do ye no remember Fontenoy, and 'Keep
front and rear thegither?'"   I wifh Mr. Davis's Ballad (Hayes's
Ballads of Ireland, vol. i. p. 213) may be as fuccefsful in fecuring
their juft fhare of credit to the fiery foldiers of the IRISH BRIGADE, for
their part in breaking and forcing back the Englifh column.

mafter. The princely pupil not only rewarded him
nobly for his inftructions, but alfo bore away a kind
remembrance of him for aftertime.

In 1747, and quite probably in confequence of
the agreeable relations formed with the Britifh officers at the Hague, Philidor made the firft of thofe
vifits to England, which he was deftined fo often
afterwards to repeat. The Englifh liked Philidor;
and as they are not hafty likers, their taking to him
fo kindly and always continuing to award him their
refpect and their patronage, is a certain proof of the
rare amiability and fubftantial good character of the
man. Here " Sir Abraham Janffen, (fays Twifs,)
introduced him to all the celebrated players of the
time.* Sir Abraham was not only the beft Chefs-
player in England, but likewife the beft player he
ever met with, after his Mafter, M. de Légal, as
the Baronet was able to win one game in four with

---

* "The beft players who were living in England, during this century, were Mr. Cunningham, Lord Sunderland, Lord Godolphin, Mr.
Cargyll, Sir Abraham Janffen, P. Stamma, Dr. Black, Dr. Cowper,
and Mr. Salvador. Moft of thefe gentlemen were to be met at Old
Slaughter's Coffee-houfe, St. Martin's Lane, in a private room."
(*Chefs*, vol. i. pp. 162–3.) Only the five laft are mentioned in any
connexion with Philidor. Cunningham, the Scholar and Jurift, was
already dead in 1730; and Cunningham, the Hiftorian, although alive
in 1735, was then extremely old. The puzzling queftion, which of
thefe *Doppelgänger* (as De Quincey calls them) is the Chefs-player's
Cunningham, appears to have been fet at reft, for the firft time, by Dr.
Irving, in his *Lives of Scottifh Writers*, (vol. ii. pp. 220–38.)

him *even:* and M. de Légal, with whom Sir Abraham afterwards played in Paris, was of the fame
opinion with regard to his fkill."*

One of the celebrated players, then in England,
was Philip Stamma of Aleppo, who was employed
by the Government as a tranflator of defpatches in
the Oriental languages.† Although he had publifhed the firft edition of his famous fituations at
Paris, it is not likely that he and Philidor had ever
met there; for in 1737, when Stamma printed his
book, Philidor was in the royal Chapel, with feveral
years of his apprenticefhip ftill before him. A
match was now arranged· between them, to confift
of ten games, Philidor giving the move, allowing a
drawn game to be a loft one, and betting five to
four on each game. The French champion loft
only two games, one of which was drawn.‡ There

---

* Count Brühl, however, makes Philidor able to give Sir Abraham
flight odds : " By all accounts, the beft player this country (England)
has produced, was the late Sir Abraham Janffen, who ufed to play on
even terms with Philidor, and to whom he could not give more than
the Pawn for the move—an advantage which amounts to little more
than the firft move." Letter to Daines Barrington, (*Archæologia*, vol.
ix. p. 14.)

† Daines Barrington, (*Archæologia*, vol. ix. and in *Chefs Player's
Chronicle*, vol. i. p. 110.)

‡ I have a warm fellow-feeling with an editor's or a biographer's
partiality for his hero; but I muft enter my refpectful proteft againft
Herr von Oppen's view of Philidor's conteft with Stamma as a conteft between *Science* and *Genius*—an encounter, in which Genius—

is no pofitive ftatement that they played any other
than thefe match-games together; but it is in the
higheft degree probable that they did; for it would
be hard to believe, that Stamma was not a frequenter, with Philidor, of the Club of gentlemen at
Slaughter's Coffee-houfe; it is expreffly ftated by
Twifs, that Stamma was one of thofe to whom
Philidor became able to give the Knight in a certain
monftrous kind of Chefs, which a Duke of Rutland
had been perverfe enough to invent, and Sir Abraham Janffen foolifh enough to delight in playing;*

---

although fhe naturally gets the worft of it—fecures more of admiration,
for the irregular brilliancy of the fight fhe makes, than her dull adverfary, for winning by mere ftolid adherence to rule and precept. Stamma's ftyle—if (as we know) his favourite game was the dry *Queen's
Gambit*—was anything but what Herr von Oppen conceives it to have
been. Nay, there is every reafon to believe, that Stamma had (par-
tially, at leaft) formed his ftyle of play in the fame fchool as his adverfary—unlefs we can fuppofe the Syrian to have lived long enough
in Paris to have publifhed a Chefs-book there, without frequenting
the *Café de la Régence* and trying his ftrength with Philidor's mafter,
M. de Légal.—(L. Bledow und O. v. Oppen, *Stamma's Hundert End-
fpiele*, p. 2.)

* " At this game, the board is fourteen fquares in breadth, and ten
in height, which makes one hundred and forty houfes; fourteen pieces
and fourteen pawns on a fide; the pawns might move either one, two,
or three fquares, the firft time. The pieces were, the *King*, the *Queen*,
then two *Bifhops*, two *Knights*, a *Crowned Caftle*, uniting the move of
the King and Caftle, and a common *Caftle*. On the other fide of
the King, was a *Concubine*, whofe move was that of the Caftle and the
Knight united, two *Bifhops*, a fingle *Knight*, a *Crowned Caftle* and a
common one. The beft players at this game, after Sir Abraham, were

and Philidor is reported to have faid, that his Chefs-
talent had been developed by playing with Stamma
—a ſtatement which could hardly have been applied
to playing a ſingle match of ten games.*

In 1748, Philidor returned to Holland, where he
compoſed his Treatiſe on Chefs. So Twiſs tells
us, briefly enough. There was much to draw him
in that direction. A brilliant campaign had opened,
in which the Duke of Cumberland, fluſhed with
his triumph over the Young Chevalier, was ſtrug-
gling in vain to hold his own againſt his brother
Chefs-player,† the victor of Fontenoy. But, whe-

Stamma, Dr. Cowper, and Mr. Salvador. Philidor, in leſs than two
months, was able to give a Knight to each of theſe gentlemen at this
game."—Twiſs, (*Chefs*, vol. i. pp. 155–6.)

* Fétis's words are: "lui-même a ſouvent dit à d'anciens joueurs du
Café de la Régence que j'ai connus, que ſon talent aux échecs s'était
développé en Hollande, en jouant avec Stamma et d'autres joueurs de
première force." The old Chefs-players were probably right in all but
the *place:* they ſpoke under the impreſſion, which they communicated
to Fétis alſo, that Philidor was in no other country but Holland, during
the whole of his reſidence abroad. Before the year 1745, however,
when Philidor left home, Stamma had become a fixed reſident of London, where he publiſhed, that very year, the laſt and complete edition
of his book, under the title of *The Noble Game of Chefs.* Nay, I do
not believe that Stamma *ever* lived in Holland at all : at any rate, the
reprint of the *Eſsai* at the Hague, in 1741, is rather evidence that he
did not, than that he did; for that reprint indicates, by its *bookſeller's*
advertiſement, that the *author* had nothing to do with it; and Stamma
indirectly, but pointedly, ignores it, in the Preface to the edition of
London, 1745.

† A proof of Marſhal Saxe's intereſt in Chefs is given by the

ther lofing or gaining ground, the Duke was ftill
attended by the friendly officers, who had crowded
around the young Frenchman's board two years before at the Hague. Aix-la-Chapelle, too, prefented
its attractions. The ftartling check, which the
Comte de Saxe had given at Maeftricht, had made
the Britifh more than willing to bring the war to a
clofe elfewhere than on the field of battle; and en-
voys plenipotentiary, with their ufual attachés and
following, were difturbing the repofe of Charlemagne
with their eager difcuffions. Here was an opportunity, not to be loft, of claiming for Chefs its proper rank among the great interefts of civilized man.
Whether Lord Sandwich, the Englifh plenipotentiary, had known Philidor in London, or not, is not
mentioned; but at Aix-la-Chapelle he proved himfelf a kind and ufeful friend. He put down his

---

"*deux Mats*" publifhed in La Bourdonnais's *Palamède,* (tome ii. pp. 41–
43,) and elfewhere. The proof, however, is not quite fo decifive as
could be wifhed; for it may be doubted whether Marfhal Saxe was the
compofer of either of the "*deux Mats*" in queftion. Both of them
belong to the clafs, known among the Germans as *Spieffruthenfpiele,*
i. e. *Running-the-gauntlet Problems,* all of which are imitations of the
ingenious original of an Italian ecclefiaftic, (Don Pietro Petronio,)
given by Salvio, (ed. 1732, p. 64.) One of them was certainly compofed by Profeffor Wildt of Caffel, (See Koch's *Codex,* vol. ii. p. 296,)
more than half a century after the Marfhal's death; and of the other,
Montigny, (who appears to have been the firft to publifh it,) merely
fays, (*Stratagèmes,* Première Partie, p. 77,) Ce coup *eft attribué* au
Maréchal de Saxe.

name for ten copies of the *Analyſe ;* and the liſt
glitters with the inſignia of other diplomatic agents,
who followed the grand Engliſhman's example at a
reſpectful diſtance. He alſo judiciouſly adviſed
Philidor to proceed to the Duke of Cumberland's
headquarters at Eyndhoven, between unlucky Mae-
ſtricht and Bois-le-Duc. The Duke played with
him, and—for Cheſs-players at leaſt—wiped out
from his eſcutcheon all the ſtains of his Culloden
campaign, by ſubſcribing himſelf for fifty copies of
Philidor's book, and by procuring a great number of
other ſubſcribers—the gallant Britiſh officers, (it
may be preſumed,) whoſe names conſtitute ſo large
a proportion of the hundred and twenty-ſeven, that
figure on the Liſt.

Philidor returned to England to carry his work
through the preſs. It was publiſhed at London, in
1749, under the title of L'ANALYSE *du Jeu des
Echecs.** Being entirely incompetent myſelf to diſ-

---

* La Borde had mentioned, that Philidor publiſhed his *Analyſe* at
London, in 1749. M. Fétis, therefore, flatly denies the very exiſt-
ence of ſuch an edition, with a reſolutenefs of ſkepticiſm, that is truly
delightful : "Outre qu'il y a bien peu de vraiſemblance qui'l y ait eu
dans la tête d'un jeune homme de vingt-deux ans aſſez d'expérience de
toutes les fineſſes, de toutes les variétés de ce jeu, pour arriver à la
clarté, à la ſimplicité des principes expoſés dans ce livre, mes recher-
ches dans les bibliographies générales, et dans les catalogues, n'ont pu
me faire découvrir cette édition de 1749." A book publiſhed in ſo
large an edition, as even the four hundred and thirty-three copies ſub-

cuſs the value of the *Analyſe* as a work of Chefs-
ſcience, I am ſingularly fortunate in being able to
refer the reader to the Eſſay on PHILIDOR *as Chefs-
author and Chefs-player*, which the great German
Maſter, Herr VON HEYDEBRAND UND DER LASA,
has done me the honour to append to my little Biography. It ſuffices for me to ſay here, that the
immediate ſuccefs of the book muſt have more
than fulfilled the moſt ſanguine anticipations of its
author. It was ſpeedily tranſlated into Engliſh and
German, and more than once reprinted in the original French, before Philidor had returned to his
native country. More fortunate than moſt didactic
compoſitions, it has ſtill retained a poſition of peculiar honour, although now, ſo far from ſtanding, as at
firſt, alone, it has fellows that are worthy to be its
peers. Even the *Theory* of the *Analyſe*—that THE
PAWNS ARE THE SOUL OF CHESS—one-ſided as it
may appear—is ſtill reſolutely maintained by one,
whoſe name is everywhere held in eſteem,—the great
Ruſſian author, Major JÆNISCH, who makes the
very title of his own palmary work (*Nouvelle Analyſe*)

ſcribed for would make, could by no poſſibility become, within a hundred years, ſuch a book as a De Bure would honour with his majuſcu-
lar RARE, unlefs the hands of Chefs-players were as deſtructive as
thoſe of the *bonnêtes artiſans* of Brunet, which have ſo nearly annihi-
lated the Elzevir *Paſtiſſier Français*. The *Analyſe* of London, 1749,
is readily ſecured by every collector : I have myſelf had three copies.

pay homage to the work of Philidor. The homage
of many others may, indeed, be unintelligent and
unreafonable, juft as the carping of fome envious
rival authors may have been uncandid and unjuft;
but I think it may be fafely faid, that the *Analyfe* of
Philidor is one of thofe "barks launched on the
Ocean of Time," that are doomed never to be en-
gulfed in its waves. It is a work of GENIUS.
Originality looks out from every page; an energetic
vitality fpeaks out from every line. Hence the
charm, which it ftill has, even for thofe who do not
wholly accept its theory.

Of this fecond refidence of Philidor's in England
it is further recorded by Twifs, that he frequented
the houfe of the French Ambaffador, the Duc de
Mirepoix, who was an expert Chefs-player, and gave
a weekly Chefs-dinner; and that in 1751, while he
was at Windfor, with the Duke of Cumberland, he
introduced Dr. Black, a clergyman, who kept a
fchool at Chifwick, as a firft-rate Chefs-player, to
the Duc de Mirepoix, at his country-houfe at Ham-
merfmith. The Doctor turned this talent to fuch
advantage, that the Duke folicited, and obtained for
him, the year following, a living of two hundred
pounds per annum, which was in the gift of the
then King, George II.

"Philidor remained another year in England, and
learning that the King of Pruffia was fond of Chefs,

he fet off for Berlin in 1751. The King faw him
play feveral times at Potfdam, but did not play with
him himfelf. There was a Marquis de Varennes
and a certain Jew, who played *even* with the King,
and to each of thefe Philidor gave a Knight, and
beat them." Such is Twifs's dry and meagre account of Philidor's vifit to the capital of the Great
Frederic. The little that can be added from other
fources is not without intereft. The celebrated mathematician, Euler—whom we may reckon among
celebrated Chefs-authors, alfo, for his algebraic
Memoir on the Knight's Tour—was, at that time,
living in Berlin. Fortunately, the mereft fragments
that fall from fuch great arithmeticians are facred;
and thus a contemporary letter of Euler's (bearing
date July 3d, 1751) has been preferved,* from which
we learn, that he too fhared in the intereft, which
was excited by the prefence of Philidor. Euler, it
feems, was a Chefs-*player*, as well as Chefs-*author*,
and would gladly have encountered the famous
ftranger over the board, but he could find no opportunity. His explanation of the caufe fhows us, that

---

* In the *Correfpondance Mathématique et Phyfique de célèbres Géomè-
tres du xviiième Siècle*, Part Firft, p. 545. The letter was ferreted
out by the Chefs-playing aftronomer, Schumacher of Altona, and
communicated by him to the Berlin *Schachzeitung* for 1848, (p. 545.)
The date of Euler's letter fhows that Twifs fhould have made 1750,
and not 1751, the year of Philidor's leaving England for Berlin.

Philidor's relations were immediately with the Court: he could not be found at Berlin, becaufe he fpent the moft of his time at Potfdam, the favourite refidence of the King.* The goffiping geometer does not forget to relate, that Philidor, *although* faid to be ftill a very young man, had feleéted a travelling companion of fuch a charaéter, that he was compelled to haften his departure, to efcape the vexatious rivalry of certain military men.†

The accurate Gerber, on the other hand, had gathered—after the lapfe of thirty years—fuch memorials of Philidor's refidence at Berlin, as proved

---

* Thirty-two years later, Philidor prefented a copy of his *Carmen Seculare* to the Prince Royal of Pruffia, afterwards King Frederic William II. The Prince's very courteous and amiable note of thanks confirms Twifs's and Euler's ftatement of Philidor's relations with perfons about the Court: " Je me rappelle toujours avec plaifir, Monfieur, quoique j'étais fort jeune alors, [feven years old,] de vous avoir vu à Berlin jouer aux Echecs avec mon inftituteur" [probably M. Beguelin.]

† Left the text fhould not be thought clear enough, I here prefent the curious reader with Euler's own German : " Er foll noch ein fehr junger Mann fein, führte aber eine Maitreffe mit fich, wegen welcher er mit einigen Officieren in Potfdam Verdrieffllichkeiten bekommen, welche ihn genöthiget unvermuthet wegzureifen." I do not believe, that Philidor "brought with him" to the Court of Frederic the Great, or took with him to the Palace of the Prince of Waldeck, any perfon of the above French-German defignation. What remains of the fcandal, after performing this fubtraétion, is likely enough (I am forry to fay) to have been true. A lively young French mufician could not be expeéted to be far in advance of his age in fuch matters.

that his Chefs-doings there had been far more brilliant than had come to the knowledge of Euler.
No other authority preferves the fact, that Philidor
exhibited his feats of blindfold playing during his
refidence abroad. Nay, it appears generally to have
been believed, that the attempt at playing more than
two fuch games at once was firft made by him at
London, fo late as 1783. But from Gerber we
learn, that in 1751 Philidor played three fimultaneous blindfold games, at Berlin, againft three fkilful players, and won them all.* The fame careful
biographer adds the important information, that
Philidor by no means fpent his time at Berlin as a
mere idle Chefs-player. In England (he fays) Philidor had gained large fums of money by the fubfcription for his Chefs-book; but in Germany he
became a gainer in another way,—in knowledge of
Mufic and of Mufical Compofition. He not only

---

* From this well-authenticated inftance, I have felt authorized to
infer, (*ante*, p. 19,) that it entered into Philidor's plans, on leaving home,
to win admiration—if not to gain emolument—by the exhibition of his
gift of blindfold playing. I have no doubt, that he did actually make
fuch exhibitions, not at Berlin alone, but alfo at the Hague, Aix-la-
Chapelle, Eyndhoven, and wherever he found any royal and princely
perfonages, or any illuftrious affemblage, to invite him. The prefents,
which he would receive on fuch occafions, would do more to keep him
above want, than his earnings from the Chefs or Draught board. The
only wonder is, that he fhould have faid nothing of the matter to
Twifs.

endeavoured to improve his tafte by liftening to the execution of *chefs-d'œuvres* in Mufic, but alfo (according to fome of Gerber's authorities) had actually ftudied under a great Mafter of the art, then refiding at Berlin.

Philidor left the Pruffian capital before the middle of the following year, and reaped the fruit of his agreeable relations with the Prince of Waldeck in 1746, by now enjoying his hofpitality for eight months at Arolfen.   After fpending three weeks at the Court of the Landgrave of Heffe-Caffel, he finally returned to England, where he remained until near the clofe of the year 1754.

Of this third refidence in England the only record that remains relates to Philidor's mufical doings. It appears, that not long after his arrival in England he appeared before the public with fome " Latin [Church] Mufic," and that he had experienced how much his more brilliant Chefs-reputation might injure him as a mufician: it was not conceived, apparently, that he could be a great Chefs-player and an original compofer at the fame time; a calumny (he complains) was, therefore, fpread about town, that he was not the author of the mufic he had given. To prove his capacity for original compofition, he now undertook to fet to mufic Congreve's Ode for St. Cecilia's Day; for it would be impoffible, he declared, for any man living to find out old mufic that

could really agree with new words.* The Ode
was performed at the Haymarket Theatre on the
31ſt of January, 1754. It was commended (according to Twiſs) by the great HANDEL. La Borde
ſays, (with more particularity,) that Handel pronounced the Choruſes to be well compoſed, but that
the ſtyle of the Airs ſtill left room for improvement.
As Handel had become blind in 1751, and rarely
went out, except to church, he could have been induced only by high regard for Philidor to have put
himſelf in the way of pronouncing this frank and
friendly opinion.† Under the encouragement of

---

* Twiſs, (*Cheſs*, vol. ii. pp. 215–17,) gives Philidor's advertiſement
in the *Public Advertiſer*, dated December 9th, 1753. Philidor, ignorant, of courſe, of Engliſh Literature, had told Twiſs in 1787, as he
had told La Borde in 1780, that the poetry, which he had ſet to muſic,
was *Dryden's* famous Ode. When Twiſs ſhowed him this advertiſement he recognized his miſtake.

† Not one word of all this does M. Fétis believe. He does not
believe, that any muſician would have been preſumptuous enough to
put new muſic to Dryden's Ode after Handel. (Twiſs's lucky diſco-
very anſwers this objection.) He does not believe, that Handel either
commended the Choruſes or found fault with the Airs, becauſe Handel no longer left his houſe. (But Hawkins uſed to ſee him in church
—and behaving himſelf very devoutly, too—during this very period.)
He does not even believe, that Philidor was in London at all during
his abſence from France. The publication of the *Analyſe* at London
does not weigh with him to the contrary, for that publication is, to him,
a pleaſant fiction and no more. Where then *was* our Philidor, ſince
he was neither in London, nor Berlin, nor in any place, that was to be
ſwallowed on the authority of the wretched La Borde? Fortunately,

a judgment fo decifive, Philidor appears to have purfued his profeffional labours with a new ardour, that
prompted him to return once more to his native
country, where, to fuch reputation as he had gained
abroad, he might add the glory of a reformer.

M. Fétis can tell us with reafonable certainty : for one M. Dunant,
the celebrated Chefs-player before mentioned, who had often played
with Philidor, told M. Fétis, in 1805, that the poor young mufician had fairly abfconded, in 1745, in order to give the flip to his
creditors, and that he lay perdu among the Dutch for nine full years,
not once efcaping from that network of dykes and canals, until he
fhowed himfelf in Paris, in 1754.

CHAPTER III.

HILIDOR returned to Paris in November, 1754, after an abſence of nine
years. He had left home a youth of
nineteen, and returned to it a man of
twenty-eight. No doubt he had ſpent a great deal
of time, during theſe nine years, in playing Cheſs ;
but, during the two laſt years he muſt have been
induſtrious as a muſician ; and that he had con-
ſtantly kept his profeſſion ſeriouſly in view is proved
by his own ſtatement to La Borde, that his taſte
had been formed, during his travels, by hearing the
great Italian maſters,—by Gerber's account of his
ſtudies in Germany,—and, above all, by the faſt,
that the ſtyle of the muſic, which he produced on
his return, gave proof both of entire change and
ſolid improvement. He found the poſt, which
Campra had vacated by death ten years before,
again vacant ; and, in order to make good his own
application for it, he produced, in the royal Chapel,

two new Motetts—one of them his *Lauda Jerufalem;* but they were confidered (fays La Borde) to
be "too Italian;" and the Queen, who took the
French fide in the great mufical controverfy of the
day, would not fuffer the ghoft of dear old Campra
to be difturbed by a fucceffor fo revolutionary.
Under thefe circumftances, Philidor, of courfe, loft
the chance of improving the mufic of the royal
Chapel and the Chefs-playing of the Pages; but he
had won the approbation of fuch as could venture
to think differently from the Court;* and, under
their encouragement, he abandoned, for the prefent, the hopelefs attempt of intruding melodious
Motetts and Anthems upon the drowfy repertory of
French Chapels and Cathedrals, and entered upon
a new career of mufical activity, which he ever
after purfued, with that cheerful induftry, which
marks the healthy and genial mind.†

---

* It is with reference (as I underftand) to the Church-mufic, which
Philidor produced at this period, that Gerber cites the following paffage
from a letter of Mereaux to the Abbé Gerbert: "Philidor, one of our
good compofers of Church-mufic at Paris, conftructs his works in the
true German and Italian ftyle, and does not, after the modern fafhion,
facrifice either Counterpoint or Fugue, or purity of Harmony, to the
mere beauty of melody."

† The "Amateurs of the Science," who (according to Twifs) com-
plimented Philidor on his improved ftyle of Church-mufic, and who
encouraged him to enter upon another career, were (no doubt) the
leaders of the fecond of the two then belligerent parties, defcribed by
Rouffeau: "L'un, plus puiffant, plus nombreux, compofé des grands,

The fact was, that the rebuff, which he had received at Verfailles, had only helped him to difcover his real vocation. He had every capacity, it is true, for the compofition of Church-mufic, but, at this moment, there was other work to be done, and he had been in training—quite unconfcioufly to himfelf —as one of the principal agents for doing it. French dramatic mufic had hitherto been little better than an engrafting of declamation upon the choral harmony of the Church, or—where lefs grave entertainment was called for—a mixture of farce and

---

des riches, et des femmes, foutenait la mufique françaife; l'autre, plus vif, plus fier, plus enthoufiafte, était compofé des vrais connaiffeurs, des gens à talents, des hommes de génie." (*Confeffions,* liv. viii.) One of thefe leaders, Diderot, was probably interefted in Philidor from the early days of the *Café de la Régence* and the receptions of La Popelinière; the other, Grimm, the friend of Diderot, was, at that time, a new-comer in Paris. André Philidor fays, that his father devoted himfelf to the mufic of the ftage by the advice of Rameau. Nothing could be more likely. We have already feen the two brought into relations with each other—and, probably, not for the firft time—in connexion with *Les Mufes galantes* of Rouffeau:—in fact, one cannot but fufpect, that Rameau aimed a fly compliment at his young friend, when he commended the Overture. Further proof of friendly relations, that might have given occafion for fuch advice, may be found in the fact, that when Rameau died, in 1767, at the age of eighty-four years, and "the *Royal Academy of Mufic,* who all regarded themfelves as his children, performed a folemn fervice in the Church of the Oratory, at his funeral, *Mr. Philidor* had a Mafs performed at the Church of the Carmelites, in honour of a man, whofe talents he fo much admired." Burney, (*Hiftory of Mufic,* vol. iv. p. 615.)

comic fong. Native agencies were only flowly
working out fome change, when, in 1752, a company of Italian burletta-fingers—called by the French
(*tout court*) *Les Bouffons*—came to Paris, and produced
a lively fenfation by their melodious and dramatic
ftyle. Jean-Jacques Rouffeau took advantage of
this fenfation to make a violent onfet upon what the
Parifians ftill clung to, in his celebrated *Letter on
French Mufic,** by which he immediately drew upon
himfelf and his fecond, Grimm, the attacks of a
legion of exafperated pamphleteers. Nothing could
have been more to his mind, than the prefent effect
and the final refult of his fudden affault. He had,
indeed, confirmed the obftinacy of the old confervative party, but he had called forth, and given a
voice to, the latent demand in the young French
mind for a mufic that fhould fpeak, with ftronger

---

* All mufical writers, from the grave Burney down to Caftil-Blaze,
appear to agree, that Rouffeau faid no more than the truth, in calling
French mufic "a clumfy pfalmody," whether they adopt, or not, his
ingenious comparifon of its *Airs* to "a galloping cow, or a fat goofe
attempting to fly." (*La Nouvelle Héloife,* 2 Partie, Lettre xxiii.) The
ftyle of finging was worthy of the mufic. "No *voce di petto,* no true
portamento," fays Burney; no *crefcendo* and *diminuendo,* no departure
from the monotony, which they "hugged," but one fteady ftrain of
the voice. Hence, when Traetta wifhed to give a certain expreffion
to the note, through which *Sofonifba* was to utter her feelings, "dans
une occafion fuprême," he could think of nothing better than to write
over the note, for the finger's inftruction, *Un urlo francefe* (a French
fcream.)—Caftil-Blaze, (*L'Opéra Italien,* p. 243.)

fympathy, to its love of mirth well paired with melody, and of natural dramatic action united with
fkilful compofition. Both of thefe parties triumphed,
each in its own way. The French party had the
Court on their fide, and therefore found no difficulty,
of courfe, in getting the poor Italians driven out of
France, in 1754, by a *de par le Roi*. The reformers
had already triumphed, when they awoke fo loud an
echo to their demand for a mufic more truly ex-
preffive and dramatic. It was neceffary, however,
that the fates fhould fecond their theoretic victory
by furnifhing them with what theory cannot produce,—the genius of the artift, to create what fhould
meet thofe afpirations, which the fkill of the difpu-
tants had only been competent to call forth, but not
to fatisfy. Imperfect attempts were making to meet
the exifting demand, and they were received with
good-will; but they were worthy only to be pre-
ludes to fomething that fhould poffefs the breath of
true poetic life.

Such was the ftate of things, when Philidor—
whofe return to France moft fignificantly bore date
the very year of the *Bouffon-hegira*—was advifed,
perhaps, by others, and certainly led by the inftincts
of his own genius, to abandon his vifions of piling
up heaps of *Glorias* and *Credos* in the library of chapels, royal or princely, and to betake himfelf to the
mufic of the ftage. His firft ftep, fo far as we know,

was (in 1757) to approach the director of the grave
and refpectable Opera of the old fchool, with a lyric
drama modeftly limited to one act. But it would
not do. The confervative M. Rébel knew his duty
better—"he would have no *tunes* on his ftage."*
Then it was that Philidor quietly turned his back
on thefe ancient refpectabilities, and entered one of
thofe homelier and more popular eftablifhments,
which had gradually grown up, from fome Bartlemy-
Fair booth (like that which Goethe has immortalized
in the Prelude to his *Fauft*) into what was now more
ambitioufly called the *Opéra-Comique*. Here it was
—at the *Foire S. Laurent*—that thofe imperfect attempts were making to realize the ideal, with which
Rouffeau and the Italian *Bouffons* had poffeffed the
minds of fuch as were fartheft removed from the
Court. A few unknown airs, compofed in 1758 for
fome unheard of *Pélerins de la Mecque*,† revealed to

---

* " En 1757, il effaya de compofer un acte d'opéra; mais Rébel
refufa de le donner, en lui difant qu'on ne voulait point introduire
d'airs dans les fcènes." (*La Borde.*) M. Fétis copies thefe words, and
then—with his cuftomary refpect for La Borde—adds " on ne fait ce
que fignifie cette phrafe." To me the fignification appears perfectly
clear.

† " En 1758, ayant fait quelques airs pour les *Pélerins de la Mecque*,"
fays La Borde. This cannot be, argues M. Fétis: " No piece of that
name was played in 1758, either at the *Opéra-Comique* or at any other
theatre in Paris." But La Borde's date of 1758 refers rather to Corbi's
offer than to the compofition which induced the offer. Again: La

the Director, Corbi—who happened not to have M. Rébel's averfion to tunes—the fact, that a rich mine of genius was offered to his hand, which he had only to work, to enrich the poor foil of his country's mufic. Philidor was immediately urged to undertake a regular comic opera. The refult was the production (in 1759) of *Blaife le Savetier*, which—although lefs perfect than fome of his fubfequent works—not only achieved a decided and permanent fuccefs for the compofer, but alfo fet the longed-for reform of dramatic mufic fairly afloat.* Our hero

---

Borde's memory may have deceived him as to the name of the piece, to which Philidor had made the infignificant contribution, and yet he may have been correct as to the fact of the contribution. That there once exifted fuch a piece as *Les Pélerins de la Mecque* appears from Fétis himfelf: he fays that Gluck once wrote mufic for it. Fétis adds, that the *Annales dramatiques* afcribe to Philidor the mufic of *le Diable à quatre*—a moft evident error, (fays Fétis,) for the fcore of *Blaife le Savetier* is infcribed *œuvre premier*. A ftrange argument, which would prove that Philidor had not written even the *Lauda Jerufalem*, which Fétis acknowledges. The fact appears to be, that Philidor had felt his way by writing feveral infignificant things, which he afterwards did not think worth mentioning or recollecting; and that the fcore of *Blaife* was marked *œuvre premier* becaufe it was his firft *publifhed* work.

* It was reprefented March 9th, 1759. "The contemporary hiftorians of the *Opéra-Comique* inform us, (fays Fétis,) that this piece was brilliantly fuccefsful. In it, Philidor fhowed himfelf to be a far more fkilful harmonift than the French compofers of his day; nay, whatever fome may fay, there was no want of melody; but his phrafing often violates dramatic truth, and his profody is very defective. There are, neverthelefs, feveral things in *Blaife le Savetier*, which predicted a

had now afcertained his true vocation, and continued to produce opera after opera, often at the rate of two a year. Of thefe I am in no condition to fpeak, otherwife than in the words of thofe who have ftudied the fcores. His fecond opera (*l'Huitre et les Plaideurs*) merely fuftained the reputation won by *Blaife le Savetier*, but in thofe, which he produced immediately afterwards, his genius (fays Fétis) took a higher flight. In each of them, particular paffages are fpecified by the fame confummate critic as not only remarkable for fome peculiar beauty, but alfo as even deferving to be looked upon with wonder, confidering the ftate of French dramatic mufic at the time. The infignificant *Maréchal Ferrant*, by the charm of its mufic alone, attained an unheard-of fuccefs : nay, it had the fingular good fortune—confidering how fpeedily the fafhion of operatic favourites paffes away—to retain its place on the ftage until fo near, at leaft, to the prefent day, that I have myfelf converfed with a mufical amateur who had heard it in Paris. It deferves to be noted, alfo, that Philidor—although a fpecial favourite of the wits, who took fides, in the *Bouffon*-war, againft the deteftable French mufic—did not win their favour by

---

brilliant career for its author, and in particular the trio, *Le reffort eft, je crois, mêlé.*" This little opera was one of thofe, which were chofen to open the new *Comédie-Italienne* with, in 1762, and continued to be a favourite for half a century.

appearing as an imitator of the Italians, any more
than of the Germans. His genius was marked—
according to the very decided expreſſion of M.
Fétis—by a charaćter totally different from that of
any of his contemporaries. Nearly every one, even
of his lighteſt comic operas, gives evidence, not
merely of originality in general, but alſo of novel
improvement in the details—ſome unprecedented
combination of the voices, ſome expreſſive ingenuity
of rhythm, ſome bold innovation in managing the
ſcanty reſources of his orcheſtra. So far, in faćt,
was Philidor in advance of his countrymen, in his
genius for inſtrumentation, that he even anticipated
ſome of the effects, which are the glory of the great
German ſchool. But favourite as he was—yet
working for his art rather than for immediate popularity—he ſometimes failed to draw forth the uſual
approbation. It was preſently ſeen, however, that
what jarred upon the popular ear at firſt, were real
beauties. *Tom Jones*, for example, which was at
firſt fairly "damned," ſoon ſecured the moſt enthuſiaſtic recognition of its merits—merits ſo great and
original, that Fétis pronounces the ſcores of *Tom
Jones* and *Le Sorcier* to be the *chefs-d'œuvre* of Philidor. Even Grimm, with all his regard for Philidor,
ſometimes complains of a new opera of his as "too
noiſy;" for ſuch was the name given to a dramatic
employment of the inſtruments, by thoſe who had

been accuftomed to hear them only as an inexpref-
five accompaniment: Philidor was "noify," in fhort,
becaufe he anticipated Gluck in making his orcheftra,
what Horace would have his Chorus, one of his
dramatis perfonæ.*

By the time that Philidor had produced his fourth
opera, (*Le Jardinier et fon Seigneur,*) his reputation
was fo high and fo firmly eftablifhed, that "he
reigned as King, in fome fort—(fuch is the ftrong
language of Fétis)—upon the fecond lyric theatre of
France." He did not, indeed, reign alone—he faw
without envy a brother near his throne, in the perfon of MONSIGNY. This melodious compofer was
a creation of the *Bouffons:* his dormant genius for
compofition was fuddenly evoked, in full power, by
hearing thefe foreign artifts fing Pergolefe's Inter-
mezzo, *La Serva Padrona,* between two ftupid acts
of fome French "ferious opera," at the *Académie
Royale de Mufique.* The fenfibility, upon which he
drew for giving foul to his melodies, was overpow-
ering even to himfelf; and by dint of an endowment
fo remarkable, although exceffively weak in mufical

---

* Orefte, dans *Iphigénie en Tauride,* dit: *Le calme rentre dans mon
âme,* et l'air qu'il chante exprime ce fentiment; mais l'accompagnement
de cet air eft fombre et agité. Les muficiens, étonnés de ce contrafte,
voulaient adoucir l'accompagnement en l'exécutant; Gluck s'en irri-
tait, et leur criait: "N' écoutez pas Orefte: il dit qu'il eft calme; il
ment."—Mme de Staël (*De l'Allemagne,* Seconde Partie, chap. xxxii.)

ſcience and technical ſkill, he enjoyed a popularity
quite equal to that of Philidor. But what could
ſuch an unfurniſhed compoſer do for the advancement of the art in France, compared with Philidor
—who, with a genius as original, had at his com-
mand all the reſources of ſcience, with the ſpirit of
invention and improvement, that marked him for a
true reformer? Between them both they ſecured
for the *Opéra-Comique*—the homely *Théâtre de la
Foire*—an aſcendency, which muſt have been infi-
nitely diſguſting to the reſpectable M. Rébel of the
dull and ariſtocratic *Académie.* Between the *Théâtre
de la Foire* and the *Académie*, however, there could
be no rivalry. Not ſo with the *Théâtre-Italien.*
That eſtabliſhment was likewiſe a dealer in comic
opera, and had, in fact, taken upon itſelf many airs
over the homelier "Fair-Theatre." But now the
tables were turned. While the Pariſians thronged
to hear the original native muſic of Philidor and Mon-
ſigny, Caillot had to ſing in Italian pieces to empty
benches; and, in the year 1762, the *Théâtre-Italien*
was obliged to come down from its arrogant poſition,
and to ſolicit and perfect an amalgamation with the
leſs dignified concern of the *Foire.* The *Opéra-
Comique* muſt have received the overtures of her
rival with the good-humour, that ſucceſs can well
afford; for, in agreeing to the name of *La Comédie-
Italienne* as that of the *amalgam*, ſhe ſurrendered half

of her own honourable title. It is to be hoped, that the *Opéra-Comique* in thus merging herſelf in the *Comédie-Italienne*, did not forget that ſhe owed her triumph, more than to any other man, to her firſt compoſer, PHILIDOR.*

---

* The portion of all this hiſtorical matter, that is perſonal to Philidor, is derived from La Borde, Twiſs, and Fétis's *Biographie Univerſelle.* For the reſt, I have alſo uſed—beſides Burney—two excellent articles of Fétis, originally written for his celebrated *Révue Muſicale,* and afterwards introduced into his *Curioſités de la Muſique.* One is entitled *De la Muſique en France,* and the other, *Sur l'Opéra-Comique.*

CHAPTER IV.

PHILIDOR IN MIDDLE LIFE.

AVING brought Philidor to this ſtage of his profeſſional career, it is proper to pauſe, for the purpoſe of chronicling two other events of his life, which may have been nearly as important in his eyes as the ſucceſs of his operas. Soon after the muſical cobbler had gladdened the merry Pariſians, the triumphant compoſer took to himſelf a wife ; but long before that time he had beaten his old maſter. When Philidor left Paris, in 1745, although he had for ſome time been playing even games with M. de Légal, and although his own name was the one great name "to conjure with," on account of his phenomenal feats of blindfold playing, he had not ceaſed to recognize his old maſter as ſtill his maſter and ſuperior. But nine years of practice, with a great variety of players, had authorized him to look for neither ſuperior nor equal ; and when, in 1755, a match was arranged between the pupil and his maſter, who was ſtill at

the height of his ſtrength, the reſult placed the crown
firmly and indiſputably upon the head of Philidor.
This, ſays Twiſs, was their laſt match. But whether they afterwards played together or not, in leſs
ſolemn encounters, they certainly retained their old
relations of friendſhip, and both continued, for many
a long year, to be the two unapproachable glories of
the *Café de la Régence.**

---

* Twiſs, (*Cheſs*, vol. i. p. 163,) writing in 1787, ſays: "Mr. de
Légalle, who is now eighty-five years of age, is the beſt Cheſs-player
in France after Mr. Philidor. The laſt match theſe gentlemen played
was in 1755, when the Scholar beat his Maſter." Légal muſt, conſequently, have been born about 1702, and, at the period of the match,
was fifty-three years old. Mr. Wálker, intending merely to copy Twiſs,
ſays in his text, "About this time he played a match at Cheſs with M.
de Légalle, and had the pleaſure of conquering his old maſter," and
continues, in a note : "At the reſpečted age of eighty-five, M. de
Légalle was ſtill the beſt player in France, always excepting Philidor."
Unhappily, Mr. Walker's words (after the neceſſary change of Twiſs's
"is" into "was") can be made to ſignify, that Légal was eighty-five,
not at the time of Twiſs's writing (1787,) but at the date of his match
with Philidor, thirty-two years earlier. Accordingly, in the wretched
Biographie of the La Bourdonnais-Méry *Palamède*, all the glory of
Philidor's vičtory over his maſter is taken away by the following per-
verſion of the Engliſh original : "Il ſe meſura alors avec ſon ancien
maître, M. de Légal, et il fut vainqueur. *Mais M. de Légal était alors
affaibli par l'âge;* il était cependant doué d'une organiſation extraordinaire, car à l'âge de quatre-vingt-cinq ans, il était encore le plus fort
joueur de France après Philidor." It may be thought, however, that
the *Palamède* is ſupported in its aſſertion, that Légal was "weakened
by age" at fifty-three, by the words of the Abbé Roman in his poem

On the 13th of February, 1760, Philidor married
Angélique-Henriette-Elifabeth Richer, daughter of a
refpeétable compofer, and fifter of three clever muficians, one of whom was long at the head of his
profeffion as a finger and teacher of finging. The
wife of Philidor, born in 1736, was alfo an excellent mufician, and is fpoken of by Gerber as ftill,
ten years after her marriage, in high reputation as a
finger at the *Concert Spirituel.**   It is a found maxim, .

Les Échecs, which is faid, in Couvret's note to the Preface, to have
been written in the year 1760 :—

> Mais Philidor eft encore dans cet âge
> Où l'on jouit de toute fa vigueur;
> Légal du temps éprouve le dommage—
> Froide vieilleffe! ainfi donc ta langueur
> Nous ravit tout, et génie et courage.
>
> *Les Échecs,* chant iv.

But, in the firft place, it is at any rate idle to fpeak of a man as
already enfeebled or chilled in his Chefs-powers at fifty-three, when
the fame man was able to beat everybody but Philidor at eighty-five ;
and, in the fecond place, the Poet was fpeaking of Philidor and Légal,
with reference—not to the match in 1755—but to a period at leaft fifteen
years later, when the former was about forty-five, and the latter about
fixty-nine—the fourth canto of *Les Échecs* having been written more
than ten years after the firft.

* The *Concert Spirituel* (fo often fpoken of in French mufical hiftory)
was inftituted in 1725 at the fuggeftion of Anne Danican-Philidor, (a
half-brother of our own François-André,) for the purpofe of furnifhing
an entertainment of religious and inftrumental mufic, at times when
it was not permitted to open the Opera-houfes. The concerts were given
in a hall of the Tuilleries. (See Fétis " *Sur le Concert Spirituel*" in his
Curiofités de la Mufique.)—[Gerber's authority was Burney, who heard

abundantly fuftained by experience, that the hap-
pieft marriages are thofe, in which the difpofition
and mental conftitution of each party forms—not
the counterpart—but the complement to that of the
other.* Philidor's marriage appears, from the fcanty
but decifive teftimony we poffefs, to have been em-
phatically of this kind. He was rather cheerfully
quiet and ferious; fhe was gay and lively. She,
again, is fpoken of as brilliant and witty in converfation; poor Philidor hardly knew if there be fuch
a thing as wit.† There are other things, however,
quite as fatisfactory, in the long run, as wit and

Madame Philidor fing a Motett of her hufband's compofition, at the
Concert Spirituel, on the 15th of June, 1770.—*Prefent State of Mufic
in France and Italy,* p. 26.]

* You may depend upon it, (fays Coleridge,) that a flight contraft of
character is very material to happinefs in marriage.—Sympathy confti-
tutes friendfhip; but in love there is a fort of antipathy, or oppofing
paffion. Each ftrives to be the other, and both together make up one
whole. (*Table Talk.*)

† The only *bon mot* recorded of him appears to have been uttered
very ferioufly, without the leaft thought of being witty. "One day,
he entered the houfe at the moment when two of his fons, of about
fourteen and fixteen, were trying their ftrength at Chefs. He looked
at their game, and after following it for two or three moves, faid to his
wife, *Ma chère amie,* our children have fairly fucceeded in making
Chefs a game of chance." (André Philidor.)—Twifs, (*Mifcellanies,*
vol. ii. p. 112,) fays, that Philidor never taught Chefs to any of his
numerous children. André's anecdote fhows, however, that Philidor
by no means prohibited his children from learning Chefs, although he
may never have chofen to teach them himfelf.

repartee. Philidor's letters prove, that he felt a lively intereſt in the current topics of the day, and that he could expreſs himſelf in reference to them with clearneſs and eaſe. There is good reaſon, therefore, to believe, that his converſation, although not brilliant, was every way agreeable and even intereſting. It appears always to have exhibited that ſimple frankneſs, which he inherited from his mother. The confidence, which ſuch a charaᒼteriſtic impreſſes upon us, that we are talking with a perfeᒼtly ſtraightforward and ſincere man, is an ample compenſation for the abſence of thoſe cold diſplays of talent, "where no heart is." The Memoirs of Grétry inform us, how perfeᒼtly *he* found the charaᒼter and conduᒼt of Philidor to correſpond with his very agreeable ſimplicity of language and manners. His wife appears ſometimes to have made a little merry with ſome of his peculiarities, but he could have underſtood nothing of her mirth but the affeᒼtion it covertly ſignified, for by no poſſibility could he be made to comprehend a joke.* The

---

* A merry relation of his, for the purpoſe of putting this negative quality of Philidor's to the proof, one day gravely expreſſed the wiſh that he were the owner of a carriage, that he might ſit at his window and ſee himſelf ride by. Philidor refleᒼted a moment, until he had analyzed the "poſition," and then remarked, "What you have ſaid there, my dear friend, is quite inconſiderate and fooliſh:—you could not be at your window and in your carriage at the ſame moment; conſequently, it would be impoſſible to ſee yourſelf ride by." (Lardin.)

fincerity of their mutual attachment, his devotion
to her and to his children, the amiable and artlefs
words and ways, in which he was wont to exprefs
that attachment and devotion, are not only preferved
in the traditions of his defcendants, but are alfo
evinced by the unpretending letters which he wrote
home from London in later years. She reminds
him, thirty years after their marriage, of the happy
13th of February, 1760; and he thanks her in return, and renews the declaration of his unabated
and tender affeɛ̄tion, in terms which make this one
homely letter worth more, in its way, than volumes
of Madame de Sévigné.*

Another joke of this kind, (among the André Philidor and Lardin
anecdotes,) is fuited exclufively to French manners, and may as well,
therefore, be given in the original : Richer, fon beau-frère, vient le
voir un matin et d'affez bonne heure : il le trouve encore couché, et
s'écrie en entrant : "Comment, ma fœur! Je vous trouve couché,
avec M. Philidor!"—"Mais, mon ami, c'eft ma femme," répond Philidor; et cette réponfe, Richer la lui a fait faire plus de cinquante fois
dans le même à-propos.

* Ce 23 Février, 1790.—Ma très-chère et très-bonne amie, j'ai reçu
tes deux lettres, et je te remercie de ton reffouvenir du jour, ou nous
nous fommes liées pour la vie. Je n'aurai rien de plus preffé que de
fonger à toi, ainfi qu'à nos enfans. Tu embrafferas deux fois notre
chère fille pour moi, et tu lui diras, que fi elle veùt me donner des
preuves de fon amitié, ce fera de ne point negliger fon piano-forte. Je
te fouhaite une auffi bonne fanté que celle dont je jouis; et je te jure
de nouveau, que je t'aime auffi tendrement, que le premier jour que
nous nous fommes connus; et c'eft avec ces fentimens que je fuis, pour
la vie, votre très-cher et très-tendre ami, A. D. Philidor.—[I am

The parties thus happily brought together were not deftined to pafs their wedded life in folitude. Sons and daughters were born to them—although not on quite fo patriarchal a fcale as the biographers would have us believe. When Twifs vifited Philidor, and made the acquaintance of Madame Philidor, at Paris, in 1783, he fell, by fome chance, into the ftrange delufion, that the then living progeny of his hoft and hoftefs amounted to nineteen *enfans terribles;* and Mr. Walker has added to the terrors of fuch a brood by printing the NINETEEN in capitals. But there were really only five fons and two daughters in all; and of thefe one of either fex died in early childhood :—the reft furvived their father.*

---

tempted to add the clofing paragraph of another letter of Philidor's (of which the autograph original is in my poffeffion) under date of London, May 17th, 1787. (It begins: *Ma très-chère et charmante amie.*) * * * * L'efpérance que j'ai de pouvoir partir dans trois femaines me fait un fi grand plaifir, que je m'ennuie beaucoup moins. Enfin, ma chère bonne amie, ce fera pour moi une fête audeffus de toute expreffion, lorfque j'aurai le bonheur de te revoir, t'embraffer, et te jurer que je ne cefferai jamais de t'aimer, et d'être pour la vie ton très-cher et très-bon ami, A. D. PHILIDOR.]

* His eldeft fon, André-Jofeph-Hélène, died June 6th, 1845, in his eighty-third year. Lardin fays he furvived all his brothers. Yet Quérard (*Supercheries,* tom. iii. p. 459) mentions another fon, Augufte Danican, (who would appear to have dropt the ancient *fobriquet,*) known as a royalift general. He was condemned to death, but efcaped, and died in Holftein, in December, 1848, eighty-five years old—which would make him born in the fame year with André. I fufpeft, therefore, that there is fome miftake here. [According to the new *Biogra-*

What flight record we have of this period indicates, that Philidor fell at once quietly into fuch a
daily routine of induftrious occupation at home, and
quiet amufement at his favourite *Café*, as comported
with his duty to his family and his profeffion, and
with the neceffity of a relaxation fuited to the character of his mind. The morning appears to have
been devoted to compofition, which he purfued in
the moft entire abforption and abfence of mind, ac-
companying his work with a perpetual twifting and
turning of his body and limbs, which his pleafant
wife ufed to defcribe by faying, that her hufband was
playing the filk-worm.   On finifhing his genial tafk,
and beginning to drefs for his walk to *La Régence*,
the thing was fometimes found impracticable for
lack of garments.   If a poor mufician had come in
upon him, during thefe hours of *robe de chambre*
abftraction, the extreme kindheartednefs and abfence of Philidor knew no refiftance to the appeal

---

phie Générale, Quérard was certainly in error—General Danican was
not a fon of Philidor's.]—The name only of another fon is mentioned
as an interlocutor in a dialogue, illuftrative of Philidor's abfence of
mind.   "Frédéric!—Papa!—Es .tu là?—Oui, papa.—Tu n'eft pas
donc forti?—Non, papa.—Eh bien! tu vas chez Marmontel, etc."—
Philidor's only daughter, Elyfe, beautiful and lively, like her mother,
at twenty-eight married Pradher, then only feventeen, who became
afterwards a diftinguifhed profeffor at the *Confervatoire*. She died in
Auguft, 1825, at the age of fifty. She was the only mufician of his
children:—none of them had any fkill in Chefs.

for charity, and precluded all diſcrimination of means. He gave whatever he could lay his hands on—coat, hat, ſhoes; and when coin could not be found in the pocket of his *culotte*, he could be prevented from giving the garment itſelf only by the watchful inter-poſition of a ſenſible maid-ſervant, to whom Madame Philidor committed the guardianſhip of the dear ſilk-worm while plying his work.

The morning taſk completed, he ſeems to have gone regularly to the *Caſé de la Régence*, and always to have taken his ſeat at the ſame Cheſs-table, over which his portrait afterwards continued to hang, until the old building itſelf was finally demoliſhed, in the barbarous ſpirit of modern improvement. At the board, Philidor became as completely ab-ſorbed as he had been at his deſk; and his medita-tions on a difficult poſition were accompanied by the ſame gyration of the body and the ſame twiſting of the limbs.* Nor do ſuch meditations appear to have borrowed any ſolemnity from ſilence. The ſtranger, who approached—and not without awe—the table of PHILIDOR, at ſome critical moment of the game, might be amazed to hear the profound Maſter of "thoughtful Cheſs" murmuring ludi-crouſly disjointed propoſitions, that gave little evi-

---

* Lardin (from André Philidor), and St. Amant, on the authority of a contemporary of Philidor's—the Chevalier de Barneville, I ſup-poſe, who died in 1842, at the age of ninety-four.

dence of any fevere logical procefs going on in his
mind.* Such filk-worm peculiarities and fuch effu-
fions of abftractednefs were, no doubt, regarded as
refpectfully here, as they were tenderly at home :—
Philidor was always and everywhere an object of
refpect, even in a circle, that embraced not a few of
thofe names, wherewith all Europe had already rung,
or was foon to ring, from fide to fide. For it was
in this fame *Café* that Voltaire liked to practife his
favourite game, whenever he lived at Paris, while
Jean-Jacques laboured perfeveringly, but in vain, to
advance one ftep beyond his firft effay, when he
gave the Rook to Bagueret. Here, at a later day,
our own Franklin diffufed the funfhine of his ever
clear and cheerful mind in the midft of the ftorm of
noife and talk, with which Frenchmen will furround
themfelves, even while playing Chefs ; and Philidor

---

* Sévelinges (*Biographie Univerfelle,* art. PHILIDOR) relates an anecdote of La Garde's taking a friend to fee his idol play Chefs, and being
obliged to account for his ftrangely foolifh talk by crying out that it
was all *genius.* This trifling anecdote is repeated by other writers,
with feveral variations, the worft of which is poor André's, who—being
a *bon vivant,* and not a Chefs-player—mifunderftood Sévelinges's word
"table," and wrote his father down as talking like a fool at the din-
ner-table (*un repas*). But Sévelinges appears merely to have been
illuftrating a habit—which Philidor had in common with many good
players—of unconfcioufly talking any kind of nonfenfe, while abforbed
in the ftudy of a difficult pofition. The newfpaper notices of his
celebrated blindfold games in London mention, accordingly, his indulg-
ing himfelf in *pleafantries* during his fevere mental labour.

had not yet ceafed to fit at his wonted table, when
Maximilian Robefpierre had begun to mingle meditations of murder and regicide with combinations for
mating the King.

The imagination fo readily pictures to itfelf the
appearance and conduct, in any fituation, of a man
fo very natural and fimple, fo amiable and fo courteous, that we do not at firft reflect, how all but defti-
tute we are of materials for continuing the hiftory
of Philidor's "familiar day." We are left to guefs,
with what deepfelt enjoyment he fat down to the
fimple meal, that awaited him, on his return from
the *Café*, by the longing he expreffed, while a daily
gueft at the tables of the great in London, for his
plain *pot-au-feu* at home. His evenings were doubtlefs fpent, for the moft part, at the Opera-houfe,
which was, in fome fort, his own ; but how he de-
ported himfelf there, in the midft of the muficians
and compofers, his friends and brothers, can only be
inferred from what we happen to know of his habitual feelings and conduct towards them under other
circumftances. When Grétry, for example, came
to Paris in 1767, with all his great reputation ftill to
make, he found Philidor not only frank and cordial
—ineapable of jealoufy towards a youthful compe-
titor for profeffional honours—but alfo active and
felf-renunciant in his friendfhip. He exerted himfelf warmly to induce the prime poet of the Opera

to give Grétry the *libretto* juſt compoſed for himſelf;
and when the conſent, at firſt granted, was afterwards withdrawn, he invited Grétry to unite his
muſic and his name with his own, now ſo celebrated,
in *Le Jardinier de Sidon*.* So his family beheld
him with awe, ſome years later, reading the ſcore of
Sacchini's ſucceſsful *Œdipe à Colone* with a ſympa-
thetic emotion, that expreſſed itſelf in ſobs and tears.
The only picture we have of him, in the theatre
itſelf, among thoſe to whom was intruſted the execution of his productions, is certainly far leſs ſolemn,
but quite as characteriſtic :—it repreſents him in
company with his handſome André, at the moment
of meeting, behind the ſcenes, a certain pretty Opera-
ſinger, (Mademoiſelle Colombe,) who had conde-
ſcended to become the boy's "firſt love"—the father bowing to the ground before her, and politely
thanking her for having taken the raw youth into
training, with the moſt innocent unconſciouſneſs of
the ſtrange confuſion, with which he was overwhelming both lad and lady, by taking ſuch parental
cognizance of their little private arrangements.†

---

* Grétry, (*Mémoires*, tome i. p. 428.)

† "Ah! Mademoiſelle, je vous remercie de vous être chargée de
mon jeune gaillard ; j'eſpère que vous en ſerez contente."—He aſtounded
another of his hopeful ſons one day, at dinner, by pulling out his watch,
and ſaying, with the moſt perfect *bonhomie:* "Partez, Frédéric; allez
mon fils; il ne faut jamais faire attendre les dames."

To complete, as far as poſſible, this very imperfect ſketch of Philidor in middle life, it is proper to
mention one or two honours conferred upon him,
with ſome account of his ſecond attempt to approach the ſame conſervative *Académie,* over which
M. Rébel had preſided as Director.

The honour, which Philidor appears to have ſet
the higheſt value upon, was "thruſt upon him,"
like Falſtaff's, by circumſtances. He had two un-
married ſiſters, who very ſenſibly provided for them-
ſelves by going into buſineſs. But in thoſe days,
no one could practice even the art and myſtery of
making millinery without being recognized, as a
maſter in the craft, by ſome appropriate guild. All
guilds, however, had ſome reaſon, good or bad, for
excluding women from maſterſhip, yet permitted
them to be repreſented by one of the rival ſex. Philidor, therefore, for his ſiſters' ſake, very eagerly
enrolled himſelf in the confraternity of Mercers—
nobody (ſays his deſcendant) can well gueſs his
reaſon for the choice; and thenceforth nothing gave
him ſo much delight as to ſign himſelf PHILIDOR,
Marchand Mercier:—nay, when he furniſhed his
name for the baptiſmal certificates of his children, it
was with this mercantile appendage.

To this period of his life we may, perhaps, refer
the peculiar honour, which he received from the
good city of Paris—that of having his buſt ordered

of Pajou. The work was executed in *terra cotta*, and was pronounced by his family to be an admirable likenefs. It was afterwards prefented by the city to Madame Philidor.* If the portrait in the Mufeum of Verfailles be a work of the laft century, that too, judging by the age reprefented, muft belong to the fame epoch. In that cafe, it was probably an honour conferred by his Sovereign, as the other had been by the city.†

The King took another occafion to diftinguifh him, in connection with his art. The fuccefs which he had gained at the *Opéra-Comique* had hitherto produced no effect upon the confervative *Académie*, or *Opéra-Françaife:*—there the old French mufic ftill reigned triumphant. He now, in 1766, had the boldnefs to aim at extending the work of reform, which had been fo popular at the *Foire St. Laurent*, to the grave fcene of the more ariftocratic Opera. With this view, he compofed, no longer a Comic but a Tragic Opera, *Ernelinde Princeffe de Norvège*,

---

* Having never feen any caft or engraving of this buft, I can only conjecture, that it may have been executed during the middle period of his life. Pajou was made Profeffor in the Academy of Painting and Sculpture in 1767, but lived until 1809.

† This portrait was lithographed for the third volume of St. Amant's *Palamède*. M. Alliey, in the firft of his interefting articles entitled *Mufée de l'Échiquier*, (*Palamède*, tome v. p. 404,) fpeaks of it as admirable; but, unfortunately, he neither gives the name of the painter, nor the date of the portrait.

"without mythology," (fays Twifs,) "and with re-
citative, after the Italian manner, intermixed with
airs." He could hardly have expected any greater
fuccefs than he actually met with. He informed
Twifs, that the Nobility, who were the laft and
moft bigoted partifans of the old French mufic,
caballed againft him; that the actors and fingers did
their beft to ruin the effect of the piece; and that
the orcheftra played their worft.* Yet Philidor's
mufic had force enough to make head againft all
this. His opera was performed for eight fucceffive
nights; and the King himfelf was fo well pleafed
with it, (fays our author,) that he privately rewarded
the compofer with a penfion of twenty-five *louis d'or*
from his privy purfe.†

---

* Philidor did not fay this, without grounds, merely to cover his
partial failure—Gluck had to encounter precifely the fame difficulties,
when he came to Paris, in 1774, to bring out his *Iphigénie*—difficulties, which to him alfo would have been infurmountable, if he had not
had the powerful fupport of the Queen, his former pupil, Marie An-
toinette. Even then, it took fix full months of rehearfal to "break
in" the perverfe fingers and muficians. All Paris daily thronged to
fee the procefs as performed by the frightful old German, who firft took
off coat and wig, then armed himfelf with a ftout cudgel for a *bâton*,
and proceeded to drill, fcold, threaten, and demonftrate, until even his
Herculean frame could ftand no more for the day. What could poor
Philidor do with a company, that could be made to do juftice to his
mufic only by a breaking-in like this?

† Of the reprefentation of this Opera, La Borde fays, it was the
epoch of a mufical reform at the *Opéra-Françaife*, and that it was the

One other piece of his fhould be mentioned—
the comic opera, *Le Sorcier**—becaufe it is in reference to it, that the charge of plagiarifm has been
made againft Philidor—and that, too, by a mean
countryman of his own. M. de Sévelinges, in the
article PHILIDOR, of the well-known *Biographie
Univerfelle*, affirms, that our compofer transferred to
Le Sorcier, note for note, a remarkable air of Gluck's
Orfeo, which had been long before reprefented in

---

model of a new ftyle, which foreign compofers (I fuppofe he means
Gluck) had only imitated after Philidor. Fétis fpeaks of *Ernelinde*
as containing beautiful chorufes, and effects of inftrumentation, which
have fince been imitated by others. It was with a view, I fuppofe, to
fome of thefe effects, that Philidor changed the compofition of the
orcheftra by introducing the novelty of another double-bafs.—Burney,
(*Hiftory*, vol. iv. p. 617,) writing in 1789, fays: "In 1770, the ferious
opera had not advanced a ftep towards perfection, or even variety, in
five years time, if the Opera of *Ernelinde*, by Philidor, be excepted, in
which that ingenious compofer quitted the ancient opera ftyle of his
country, accelerated the recitatives, and terminated his fcenes with
many excellent airs, *à l'Italienne*." Scudo fays, in 1858, "The chorufes
of *Ernelinde* are ftill celebrated"—one of them (*Jurons fur ces glaives
fanglants*) having been incorporated into the current oratorio of *Saül*.
(Caftil-Blaze, *De l'Opéra*, tome ii. p. 130.)

   * According to Caftil-Blaze, *Le Sorcier*, in other refpects a *chef-
d'œuvre*, contained an amufing fpecimen of Philidor's comic humour:—
"Dix ans après, [he is fpeaking of the *Bouffon* war,] le 2 janvier, 1764,
Philidor égayait les habitués de la *Comédie-Italienne* en leur préfentant
la caricature du chant français de cette époque. Dans la fcène d'évo-
cation du *Sorcier*, Caillot imitait les acteurs de l'Opéra d'une manière
très-plaifante." (*L'Opéra-Italien*, p. 150.)

Italy. A ftill meaner Frenchman adds the affertion,
that Philidor had contrived to get poffeffion of the
fcore of the *Orfeo*.* M. Fétis more than makes up
for all his fkepticifm, by his trenchant expofure of
this recklefs attack upon the probity of Philidor.
His anfwer is, *Firſt*, Gluck's *Orfeo* was played, not
in Italy at all, but at Vienna, in July, 1764, while
Philidor's *Sorcier* was played at Paris, on the 2d day
of January, *fix months earlier*, and, *Secondly*, M.
Fétis had read the fcores of both pieces, and had
found that there was not a fingle phrafe common to
both.† This fame Gluck was the one, who was
deftined afterwards to perfeét that reform of the
ferious opera, in which Philidor's fuccefs had been
only partial; yet fo far was either of thefe great
men from any envy or jealoufy of the other, that,
upon fome occafion, when Gluck, being obliged to
abfent himfelf from Paris, needed the affiftance of
fome competent and friendly brother in the art to
fuperintend the repetition of this fame *Orphée*, (in

---

* [There appears to have been another and an earlier calumniator
in the cafe. According to M. Fétis, the charge of plagiarifm originated
with Favart, the dramatic poet.]

† " C'eft cependant (writes M. Fétis with juft indignation) de cette
anecdote que l'auteur de la *Biographie univerſelle et portative des contemporains* eft parti pour refufer le génie de la mufique à Philidor, et le
repréfenter comme un homme qui ne vivait que de plagiats, tandis que
le talent de ce compofiteur a un caractère abfolument différent de tous
fes contemporains."

its French drefs,) he left his fcore in the hands of
Philidor, who directed the rehearfals with as much
attention and intereft as if the piece had been his
own.*

---

* Such is the only way in which I can make anything fatisfactory
out of André Philidor's ftatement, that his father fuperintended the
rehearfals of the *Orphée* in 1774—the very year of Gluck's firft arrival
in Paris, when he certainly brought out his Opera under his own eye.
But between 1774 and 1779 Gluck once, at leaft, (and probably more
than once,) returned to Vienna; and André's ftory appears to be in
fome fhape entitled to belief: *Firft*, becaufe it is a family tradition, not
likely to be entirely without foundation, and, *Secondly*, becaufe it contains one fact, in common with the fecond of the two flanders, viz.,
the poffeffion of Gluck's fcore by Philidor.

CHAPTER V.

PHILIDOR AND THE LONDON CHESS-CLUB.

FOR nearly twenty years had Philidor been thus purfuing the even tenor of his profeffional labours, when, in 1772, the current of his remaining years received a new direction. "This year," (fays Mr. Twifs,) "he came to England, and paffed a month with his friends." It feems, however, hard to believe, that Philidor, at the age of forty-fix—after the wandering fpirit of his youth had been, for eighteen years, thoroughly laid and fmothered by wife and children and profeffional fuccefs—fhould have fuddenly undertaken, of his own accord, to vifit a fcene, from which the moft of his old friends, ftout Sir Abraham, dark Stamma, and their contemporaries, muft have long fince difappeared.* It is

---

* Sir Abraham Janffen died, Feb. 19th, 1765, at Paris, where he appears to have been living for feveral years. [Twifs's date of 1763 is probably not fo much a miftake, as a mifprint.] Some account of him may be found in Nichols's *Anecdotes*, (vol. iii. pp. 406–11.)—When

far more likely, that Philidor was drawn from his regular and induſtrious way of life by a ſpecial and preſſing invitation.   A younger generation of ama-teurs had grown up in England, that ſeemed dis-poſed to aim at being "better than their fathers." In 1770, a new Club, at the Salopian Coffee-houſe, had ſuperſeded the heroic rendezvous of Old Slaugh-ter.   Count Brühl, on whoſe boyiſh path we have ſometimes fancied that the light of Philidor's coun-tēnance may have fallen in 1752, had now been for ſeveral years reſident in England, where, in 1767, he had married an Engliſh wife.*   Now, we know that he occaſionally viſited Paris ;† and we may be certain, that he did not viſit Paris without viſiting all that made Paris Paris to a Cheſs-player—the *Café de la Régence* and Philidor.   May it not, then,

---

Stamma publiſhed his *Noble Game of Cheſs*, in 1745, he informed the public, that "no Copies o the Book were genuine, but ſuch as were ſign'd by him."   The copies, which have this ſignature are very rare. It may, therefore, be inferred, that Stamma died pretty ſoon after the publication of this edition—or, at any rate, long before the whole of it had been diſpoſed of.

* John Maurice, Count Brühl, Envoy of the Elector of Saxony, at London, was born Dec. 20th, 1736, and died Feb. 22d, 1809, aged 72.   He would, therefore, have been about fourteen or fifteen in 1752, when I have ventured to think a viſit of Philidor's to Dreſden poſſible. According to the *Gentleman's Magazine*, on the 6th day of July, 1767, Count Brühl was married to the Counteſs-dowager of Egremont.

† In his Letter to Daines Barrington (*Archælogia*, vol. ix.) he uſes the expreſſion "during my laſt viſit to Paris."

be a moſt reaſonable, and by no means a fanciful,
conjecture, that the invitation of Count Brühl, in
behalf of the enthuſiaſtic amateurs whom he repreſented, had ſomething to do with this "coming to
England and paſſing a month with his friends?"*

Be this, however, as it may, the preſence of Philidor ſeems to have renewed the demonſtration, that
there was ſomething in his character, independent
of his talents, that had a peculiar charm for the
Engliſh mind. It was the league between Kwaſind
and Chibiabos again. The "very ſtrong" Engliſhman loved and reſpected the "gentle" Frenchman,
doubly rich in faculties, which he bore ſo meekly—
amiable in ſociety, but with a ſingle heart for his
loved ones at home—generous, yet ſelf-denying and
provident, and of a life ſtainleſs in its purity and in-
tegrity. A month's enjoyment of his preſence, ſo
agreeable and ſo inſtructive, proved to be what the
Engliſh players would not willingly be without:—
having had it once, they wanted it again and always.
Now, what the Engliſh like they will have; and
could they have got poſſeſſion of Philidor, with his

---

* [Philidor's intereſt in the Cheſs-playing circles of London may
have been kept alive by two other cauſes, namely, the continued preſence of Sir Abraham Janſſen, at Paris, and the occaſional viſits of
other native amateurs—for his acquaintance with Engliſhmen lay very
much with thoſe who were beſt able, and quite likely, to indulge them-
ſelves in a trip to the moſt attractive of foreign capitals.]

golden mines of Chefs-fkill, in no other way, I make
no doubt they would have *annexed* him by the ftrong
hand, like fome Scinde or Oude of remote Hindo-
ftan; but fortunately it occurred to them to try
what liberal offers would do, along with permanent
arrangements for making thofe offers effe&ual.   In
1774, therefore, they formed a new Club in St.
James Street, under the very fhadow of the Palace.
The number of members was limited to a hundred :
—the terms of fubfcription, three guineas.   The
evidence of fome ftrong impulfe and of fome fpecial
obje&, in forming this Club, may be found in the
chara&er of its original members.   It was no mere
private affociation of quiet Chefs-players : ftates-
men, warriors, men of letters—all crowded forward
to enter its ranks; infomuch that when Gibbon
came to town, refolved to play a part in high life,
he joined the new Chefs-club as one of the "*fafhionable Clubs.*"   One noble lady, Dr. Franklin's Mrs.
Howe,* ftood by the fide of a Church dignitary, the
Bifhop of Durham,† at the head of a lift, on which

---

* An interefting account of this lady, of whofe "difcretion and excellent underftanding" Dr. Franklin formed fo high an opinion, may
be found in Mr. Fifke's paper on the "Chefs-life of Benjamin Franklin," in the *Book of the Firft American Chefs-Congrefs*, pp. 331–39.

† The "Golden See" was at this time held by John Egerton, father
of the Hon. Francis Egerton, (afterwards Duke of Bridgewater,) in
whofe houfe, at Paris, (in 1807,) the curious confultation-games were

—befides uncounted Dukes, Marquiffes, and Earls —were found the hiftorical names of Charles James Fox and Lord Mansfield, of Erfkine, Wedderburne, and the Marquis of Rockingham,—of Elliot, the defender of Gibraltar,—of Frafer, who met a foldier's death, and Burgoyne, who underwent a foldier's laft humiliation, at American Saratoga.

The firft ftep of the new Club was to provide, that a fubfcription fhould be annually made amongft its members, to be offered to Philidor, as an inducement to him to fpend the *Seafon* of every year in London—a period which at that time covered the four months from February to June.* There could have been no refifting fo liberal an offer, made by fuch men, actuated by feelings fo friendly and refpectful. His acceptance of the offer would not of neceffity interfere ferioufly with his labours, or leffen his emoluments, as a mufician, while it would be materially increafing his income at a moft opportune moment, when the age of his fons muft have begun to demand increafed expenditure on his part. Thefe confiderations were weighty enough to overcome the reluctance which he muft have felt, at feparating himfelf, for fo large a part of every year, from a

---

played, in connection with which the name of DESCHAPELLES is firft heard of.—(*Chefs Monthly*, vol. ii. pp. 58–59.)

* This is afcertained from his letters. The earlieft date is in February; in one he fays he cannot be in Paris until the 20th of June.

home, to which he clung fo tenderly; and, in 1775, he fpent his firft feafon in London, under the new arrangement.

There are circumftances which tend to fhow, that the confiderate kindnefs of Philidor's Englifh friends did not end with providing him a falary. The publication of the new edition of the *Analyfe*, in 1777, appears to have been promoted by them, with a view to put into his hands an extraordinary fum at the beginning of his connection with the Club. The edition itfelf was dedicated "to the very illuftrious and honourable Members of the Club," and the name of every member, without exception, appears upon the Lift of Subfcribers. The perfonal exertion of the members to enlarge the Lift is evinced by the character of the names which were added to their own. We can fancy the Scotch Duke of Athol getting the name of the Scotch Duke of Argyle, and Charles Fox bantering Lord North into putting down his guinea. Gibbon, with his courtly fmile and the tap on his fnuff-box, may have won the fupport of Lady Di Beauclerk; and the activity of dear Mrs. Howe fhall have (in my mind) the credit of fo many of the fifty noble ladies, as did not fubfcribe in obedience to their hufbands. As the French names do not exceed fifty— although thefe form a brilliant array—the inference is a very clear one, that the edition was efpecially an

affair of the Englifh Club, and connected with their
arrangements for the perfonal emolument and gratification of the author.*

Of the habits and occupations of Philidor, during
thefe annual refidences in London, we catch no
glimpfe, until about fifteen years after the arrangement had gone into operation. Eight familiar letters, written between the years 1787 and 1790,
enable us to form a pretty clear idea of the amiable
old man's day in London, and to conjecture what it
may have been, when greener years and better health
permitted him to accomplifh more. We find him,
at paft fixty, in refpectable lodgings,† devoting a
portion of his time—probably the morning hours,
as at home—to mufical compofition,‡ or amufing
himfelf with a walk and goffip with friends, as every
Frenchman, and moft reafonable men, will do. He
meets the Abbé Vogler, and they try a new piano;

---

* There were two hundred and eighty-three fubfcribers, and three
hundred and fixty-feven copies, in all. The French names are under
fifty. Among them are thofe of *Monfieur*, (afterwards Louis XVIII.,)
who was fubfequently the head of the Parifian Chefs-Club,—of Philidor's old mafter, Légal,—of Dukes, Marquiffes, Counts, and Marfhals
many,—and of Marmontel, Raynal, Diderot, and Voltaire.

† " Notre mylord Goy eft à Londres, et loge dans la même maifon
que moi." (*Letter*, Feb. 20th, 1788.)

‡ " J'avance dans mon ouvrage, et je fuis très-content de mes idées.
—Je compte que je reviendrai, avec tous mes brouillons de la totalité
de mon ouvrage: j'ai la plus grande envie de prouver que la vieilleffe
ne m'a pas encore éteint le génie." (*Letter*, April 22d, 1789.)

he falls in with M. de Calonne, who preffes him to join him at dinner.* When not thus appropriated by fome fpecial invitation, he goes where he has a ftanding engagement—to his friend, Count Brühl's. Then both go to the Club, where Philidor finds his regular occupation.† Occafionally, he brings out before a London audience fome of his compofitions, and then he miffes the help and voice of his faithful Richer.‡ At another time, we hear of him at a party, where admiffion could be gained only by talent and character.§ And fometimes, there is

---

* *Letters*, February and March, 1790.

† "Je ne m'amufe que lorfque je fonge à toi: je n'ai point encore été à aucun fpectacle. Je me promène le matin, et vais diner chez le Comte de Brühl, et de là à notre Club. Voilà, à peu près, la vie que je mène." (*Letter*, Feb. 20th, 1788.)

‡ "Mon *Carmen* a été très-bien reçu, mais Richer me manquait." (*Letter*, June 3d, 1788.)—"J'ai reçu mon *Te Deum*—je vais chercher à pouvoir en faire ufage." (*Letter*, March 20th, 1790.) Gerber (*Hiftorifch Biographifches Lexicon*) fays, that Philidor ufually gave a Concert of his vocal compofitions during each of his London vifits, and that (*as they fay*) he ufed to gain from each concert *two hundred guineas*. Of courfe, an exaggeration.—I may add, that as Philidor played no inftrument, he depended upon his wife and her brothers— Louis Richer, the teacher of finging, efpecially—for trying the effect of any vocal pieces, which he happened to be compofing.

§ Mr. Staunton tells the following anecdote, in Tomlinfon's delightful *Chefs-Player's Annual for* 1856, (p. 160.) "Madame d'Arblay (Mifs Burney that was, you know) once told me, that Philidor was at one of her parties; and when fhe afked him to play at Chefs, he replied: 'Madame, I am not prepared.'—'How fo? I thought, Mon-

reafon to think, the folitarinefs of his London refidence was relieved by the fociety of his wife and daughter.*

We have no means of afcertaining, with exactnefs, the income which Philidor derived from his engagement with the London Club. It does not appear whether the fubfcription, which was annually renewed, was always for the fame amount.† At

---

fieur Philidor, you were always ready to play at Chefs." "Pardon, Madame; when I play at Chefs, I do not dine until I have done playing, and to-day I have already dined."—Mifs Burney did not marry General d'Arblay until two years before Philidor's death. It is, therefore, uncertain, whether "her parties" were given at her own, or at her father's, houfe, and whether fhe invited Philidor as a diftinguifhed compatriot of her hufband's, or as an ornament to the profeffion of her father. In any cafe, admiffion to her parties was an honour.—As to the anecdote itfelf, I would obferve : Philidor, as we have feen, did all his playing at the Club *after* his dinner with Count Brühl. It is, therefore, clear that he muft have underftood Madame d'Arblay as afking him to give the company a fpecimen of his *blindfold playing.* For that, he *did* fometimes prepare himfelf by obferving a careful regimen for feveral days; and the hour mentioned (Twifs, *Chefs*, vol. i. p. 168, and *Mifcellanies*, vol. ii. p. 109) for two of his exhibitions, and probably for all, was two o'clock. The dinner of the Club followed.

* Je ne perds point de vue ton voyage, avec ma fille, l'hiver prochain; et je ne doute aucunement, que tu ne regrettes, autant que moi, de n'avoir pas voulu me fuivre. (*Letter*, March 20th, 1790.)

† Upon the whole, however, fince both Philidor and Twifs fpeak of the fubfcription as raifed "for defraying Philidor's expenfes," it may be inferred, I think, that fuch expenfes were reckoned, from the firft, at fome round fum; and that it only remained for the individual members of the Club (who never remained the fame for any length of

one time he fpeaks of having already fent home about feventeen hundred *livres* of it (nearly three hundred and twenty-five dollars;) at another, of fifteen *louis* (fixty odd dollars) being ftill due. It is more important to note, that Philidor appears always to have calculated on fending every penny of this falary to his family, and on fupporting himfelf by the other gains, which he had the opportunity of making.* Thefe muft have been derived, *firft*, from the ftakes, for which Chefs has always been played in England, and which, in his cafe, muft have been treated as fees for inftruction; and, *fecondly*, from the admiffion-tickets to his exhibitions of blindfold playing. As no one was known to poffefs that remarkable power before Philidor, and as no one arofe in his day to fhare the poffeffion with him, it was looked upon as a unique phenomenon; and the opportunity for obferving it was eagerly fought for by the fcientific and the curious. Under thefe circumftances, his friends of the Club made various arrangements, from time to time, to render the exhibitions of Philidor's blindfold playing a means of adding to his emolument. We are dif-

---

time) to determine what fhare of this fum each would fubfcribe. I fufpect that Gerber's *on dit* refers to Philidor's *falary*, and not to the profits of his concerts.

* "Mon plan eft de vivre au dépens de mes petits profits, et de me donner les chofes, dont je pourrais avoir befoin, et d'épargner entièrement ma foufcription." (*Letter*, Feb. 20th, 1788.)

tinctly informed, for example, by one of his letters, written in February, 1790, that at the Club-dinner, which followed the firft exhibition of the feafon, it was fettled by vote, on motion of General Conway, that there fhould be a dinner, preceded by a blind-fold match, every other Saturday. What might otherwife have appeared an undignified private fpe-culation, was made every way refpectable by the direct patronage and countenance of the diftin-guifhed gentlemen, who compofed the affociation; the advertifements were dated, and the games played, in their rooms; and the members appeared as pri-vileged fpectators. It is not probable, however, that precifely fuch exhibitions as thefe were given, or that they were put on fuch a footing, until fome years after Philidor's arrangement with his Englifh friends in 1775. Diderot's friendly remonftrance with him, in 1782, for perilling the talents and glory of a Pergolefe in a *tour de force* more fuited to a Greco, unlefs with the profpect of great pecuniary advantage, implies that exhibitions of *three* games were then a novelty, and that no exhibitions had been hitherto paid for. Twifs fpeaks of his having played two public matches in 1783 and 1788, and four in 1789. It was not, therefore, as it would appear, until after the frefh enthufiafm, with which Philidor was at firft welcomed, had paffed away, and the overflowing ftream of Englifh bounty had gradually fhrunk to its natural channel, that his friends encouraged him to avail himfelf of the enduring intereft in the difplay of his unique powers, to make good the falling off in his earlier income. But the revenue from this fource, too, muft have gradually fuffered fome diminution, and then the exhibitions were made more frequent. If it be true, that when Diderot remonftrated with him in 1782, Philidor's emolument from his blindfold playing amounted to fcores or even hundreds of guineas a feafon, then it fpeaks loudly for his unexacting moderation of character, that in 1790—at a time when only fifty-fix fubfcribers encouraged the third edition of his *Analyfis*,* and when he was exerting himfelf beyond his ftrength for his family†—he fhould

---

* A fubfcription-lift fo fmall, compared with that of the fecond edition, only proves that the Club had ceafed to be a fafhionable affociation, organized for the accomplifhment of a certain object, and that it had now become a quiet Chefs-Club, and nothing more. There were few members to fubfcribe or to folicit fubfcriptions, and no motive for making another extraordinary effort. So reduced had the members become, that when fourteen had affembled at the firft dinner of the year 1790, Philidor informed his wife, that the feafon would be a brilliant one. That the Club retained all their regard for Philidor undiminifhed was teftified that very year by the purchafe of his portrait by Robineau for their rooms—"et me voilà (he writes to his wife) *pendu* dans notre falon d'échecs à Londres!"

† "J'apprends, avec grand plaifir, que mes enfans pourront être placés; et réelment j'en ferais bien enchanté, attendu que je furpaffe mes forces dans ce moment."—(*Letter*, March 20, 1790.)

ſpeak to his wife of eight *louis** profit from his firſt
exhibition as a moſt ſatisfactory reſult, without one
word of complaint—without one backward glance
at the golden ſhowers of a few years before. In
fact, the profit and loſs account ſeems to have
weighed leſs with him, than the pleaſure he took
in the exerciſe of his rare gift, and in the expreſſions of delight and wonder, which it never failed
to call forth.† The "enchantment" of the ſpecta-
tors was regularly echoed by the preſs, from the
periſhable newſpaper ſheet up to the permanent
record of the *Annual Regiſter* itſelf.‡

---

* Twiſs (*Miſcellanies*, vol. ii. p. 109) gives Philidor's laſt advertiſement, dated "Cheſs Club, 1795." The price of tickets was then
five ſhillings. In 1790, it was probably the ſame, for forty-three
tickets gave him the eight *louis* clear profit.

† "Il y a des éloges étonnants dans toutes les gazettes, au ſujet des
trois parties ſans voir que j'ai jouées ſamedi dernier. Ils diſent, que la
netteté de mes idées augmente avec mes années. Il eſt vrai, que
jamais je n'ai eu la tête auſſi nette." (*Letter*, June 3, 1788.) "J'ai
joué ſamedi dernier mes trois parties à la fois—tout le monde a été
dans l'enchantement." (*Letter*, Feb. 1790.)

‡ Were not the *Palamède* a recogniſed Cheſs-claſſic, it would hardly
be worth while to ſay anything more, than I have ſaid already, (*antè*,
pp. 10, 11,) of its errors in reference to theſe blindfold exhibitions of
Philidor. Perhaps *all* of them are ſufficiently refuted by the ſtatement, that they emanate from the brilliant poet and noveliſt, M. Méry,
whoſe devotion to *biſtorical* accuracy may be eſtimated by his off-hand
way of diſpoſing of Philidor as an *émigré*, who died (*be rather thinks*)
in 1795—("il eſt mort, je crois, en 1795.") *Some* of them, at all
events, carry the character of pure and pleaſant fiction upon their very

Such were the occupations of Philidor, during his yearly vifits to the Britifh capital.*   The tenor

face.   When, for example, M. Méry fays, that Philidor ufed to give *Soirées* of [only] *one* or *two* blindfold games at a time, in London; that, by taxing the opulent Englifhmen *a guinea* a head for admiffion, he made money enough to compofe operas at his leifure, and to *give leffons in Chefs* to Jean-Jacques Rouffeau; and that Jean-Jacques [in fpite of fuch inftruction] was a weak player, but did not *confefs* the fact in his *Confeffions*—who does not fee, that, as the laft of thefe carelefs affertions was made for the joke's fake, with full knowledge that it could be confuted on the fpot by opening the book, fo all the reft are thrown out, with the moft entire unconcern, whether the reader fhall take them for abfolute *fabrications*, or merely for wild *exaggerations*?   *One* of M. Méry's random fhots does, indeed, borrow fome appearance of approaching the mark, from Philidor's adopting a regimen before playing—namely, the ftatement, that when Philidor, on juft *three* occafions in his life, [precife M. Méry!] played *three* fuch games at once, his faculties were fo completely exhaufted, that he was unable, for a long time, to collect his thoughts again.   M. Méry, however, appears to have had no other authority for faying this, than Diderot's letter.   But Diderot betrays no knowledge of *Philidor's* having actually experienced any fuch exhauftion : he is merely attempting to frighten Philidor with the apprehenfion, that he *might* exhauft his faculties, inafmuch as *M. de Légal* had fuffered the moft alarming proftration from playing only *one* game without the board.   The truth is, M. Méry *really* drew his picture from poor La Bourdonnais—as appears clearly enough from a half-recantation in *La Régence* for 1851, (p. 131.)   Philidor can have fuffered no extraordinary fatigue, or it would have been phyfically impoffible for him to give his blindfold *Soirées* once a fortnight, through the feafon; nor would he have written, as he did, to his wife, in 1790, with the weight of fixty-four years upon him : " Je t'affure, que cela ne me fatigue pas autant que bien des gens peuvent le croire."

* That Philidor really enjoyed living in England for fomething be-

of his life at home, during the remaining two-thirds
of each year, was undoubtedly influenced by his
new arrangements, as well as by other caufes, which
were coming into operation at about the fame time,
but by no means in fuch a manner, as to juftify the
very unfavourable—not to fay very harfh—ftate-
ments of certain thoughtlefs French writers, who
have haftily applied to the whole of his later years
the cenfure, which M. Fétis has too haftily applied
to the period from 1785 to his death. While M.
Scudo, for example, has fimply copied Fétis, with
no diftruft of his accuracy, M. Adam—the pleafant
writer as well as charming compofer—has reprefented Philidor as merely trifling with his profeffion,
and as giving to Mufic only fo much time as he
could fpare from Chefs.* But it is certain, that

---

fides the money it brought him may be fairly enough inferred from
the following anecdote in the later edition of Dibdin's *Bibliomania,*
(1842, p. 612)—"William Templeman, of Hare Hatch, Berkfhire,
was a great Chefs-player. . . . . He faid, that he once fat on Philidor's knee, who patted his cheek, and told him 'there was nothing
like Chefs and *Englifh roaft beef.*'" But he did *not* tell Mr. Templeman, what I dare fay Twifs had to extort from him, and then was
mean enough to repeat—"Among the *Ladies* he has not met with a
firft or even fecond-rate player." (*Chefs,* vol. i. p. 165.) I call my
fair readers to witnefs, that—fo far from adopting this piece of malice
into my text—I have degraded it to the foot of the page, and have
condemned it to the infignificance of *Brevier.*

* "Un feul compofiteur, depuis Rameau, avait obtenu un fuccès
décidé à ce théâtre, [the *Opéra-Français,*] c'était PHILIDOR avec fon

both M. Adam and M. Scudo, and he whom they have followed, M. Fétis, have fpoken under very erroneous impreffions of the real facts of the cafe.

From 1759 to 1775—from the compofition of *Blaife le Savetier* to his engagement with the Englifh Club—the feries of Philidor's mufical productions had been unbroken. It would not have been furprifing, nor even particularly cenfurable, if now —after fo many years of labour, and upon the approach of old age—he had been tempted, by the large fums he had received from the fubfcribers to his book, and by his regular annual falary, to confider his profeffion as fubftantially changed, and to have indulged himfelf in a refpite from the exciting and exhaufting toil of mufical compofition. And if, with fuch a view of what was henceforth to be his fpecial avocation and fureft refource, he had fpent more hours than before at the *Café de la Régence,*

Ernelinde; mais ce compofiteur femblait ne prendre fon art que comme un délaffement; ce qui était férieux et important pour lui, c'étaient les échecs, et ce n'eft que dans les moments perdus que lui laiffait fon jeu favori, et pour fe repofer des fatigues que lui caufaient les combinaifons de l'échiquier, qu'il confentait à s' occuper de fes opéras." (Adam, *Derniers Souvenirs d'un Muficien,* p. 183.)—It is a pity that the lateft and ableft eulogift of Philidor, M. ARTHUR POUGIN, fhould have been equally mifled, with Adam and Scudo, by the authority of Fétis. M. Pougin's noble rehabilitation of his countryman, in the *Revue et Gazette Muficale de Paris,* (for Sept. 11th and 25th, and Oct. 2d, 1859,) was made without any fufpicion, that a ftranger had taken the initiative in the fame good work.

to keep himſelf in full ſtrength as a Cheſs-player, who could reaſonably maintain, that he was not in the way of profeſſional duty? But Philidor did not ſo reaſon, nor did he ſo conduct himſelf. When he returned from his firſt ſeaſon in England, with hundreds of guineas in his pocket, his firſt thought appears to have been, that he could now achieve ſomething greater in muſic, than the neceſſity of providing for conſtantly-returning wants had permitted him to do before. One act operas, ſpeedily compoſed for a ſpeedy return of profit, no longer anſwered to his profeſſional aſpirations. Beſides, he was now no longer maſter of the field, which for twenty years had been almoſt excluſively his own. A new ſtar had riſen—not to diminiſh the luſtre of his—but to divide with it the admiring gaze of the public. The operas of Grétry were now an attractive novelty; and Philidor—although his pieces ſtill kept the ſtage and ſtill elicited the warmeſt applauſe—was not ſo preſſed by the Directors for new compoſitions, as he had been before, nor could he feel the ſame motive for haſtening a freſh appearance.* He deliberately turned his attention, there-

---

* [How rapidly the operas of Grétry were produced, and with what ſucceſs they were exhibited, at both the *Opéra-Français* and the *Comédie-Italienne*, appears from the *Mercure Français*. The Publiſher and Editor of this periodical, Lacombe, was the brother-in-law of Grétry: it was natural, therefore, that he ſhould be ready enough to extol the compoſitions of his relative, eſpecially when he had all Paris on his

fore, to another department of profeffional labour. He took as his theme the *Carmen Seculare* of Horace. So far from being deterred by the difficulties of wedding a charaᶜteriftic produᶜtion of ancient Pagan Literature to an art, that bears almoft exclufively the ftamp of modern Chriftian cultivation, he appears to have grappled with his tafk as one that would enable him to do juftice to his genius and his fcience. Upon this tafk he worked flowly—but, to all appearance, affiduoufly—for two or three years; yet not with fuch entire abjuration of his dramatic career, but that he alfo compofed an elaborate Lyric Tragedy, his *Perfée*, during the fame period. The *Carmen Seculare* was firft brought out at London, in the year 1779, and afterwards at Paris. The great fuccefs, which it met with, attraᶜted the attention of Catharine of Ruffia: fhe requefted a copy of the fcore, and rewarded the compofer with imperial munificence.* The *Perfée* was brought out at the

---

fide. The tone of decided refpeᶜt and admiration, with which Lacombe everywhere fpeaks of Philidor, may be taken as reprefenting the feeling of Grétry himfelf.]

* Gerber fays "600 Liv." (Pounds fterling, I hope, and not *Livres Tournoi*.)—It was performed three nights (fays Twifs) at Freemafon's Hall. In 1788, it was again brought out in London, at an entertainment given by the Knights of the Bath. (Burney, in Rees's *Cyclopædia.*) It was then publifhed at Paris, "dedicated to the Emprefs, with an engraven title-page, reprefenting the arms of Ruffia." (Twifs.) It appears, moreover, from a letter of Philidor's, (June 3, 1778,) that it

Opéra-Français in 1780. Two other dramatic compofitions, one of which muſt have been the fubjeƈt of long and careful ſtudy, occupied the time of Philidor for the next four or five years:—the grand opera of *Thémiſtocle* was reprefented at Fontainebleau, in prefence of the Court, in October, 1785; and a few days later *L'Amitié au Village*, in one aƈt, was brought out at the *Comédie-Italienne.* The tragic piece was remarkable for elegance of ſtyle and originality of inſtrumentation, but did not produce ſo much effeƈt as its lighter companion, which excited ſo lively an enthuſiafm, that the audience called for the compofer—an honour at that time almoſt without precedent.*

---

was publiſhed by fubſcription—the greater part of the fubſcribers (I will venture to fay) being Engliſh.—Catharine addreſſed her application and acknowledgments to Philidor through his friend Grimm. "Cette grande Princeſſe," he writes, "ne ſe borne pas à vouloir entendre votre ouvrage en concert; elle a fait écrire à un des plus célèbres favants d'Italie, pour lui demander un programme, afin de relever le charme de votre muſique par la pompe du ſpeƈtacle et la repréſentation exaƈte des cérémonies réligieuſes, qui vous ont infpiré." The heir-prefumptive of Frederic the Great acknowledged the receipt of the *Carmen Seculare* in MS. by a letter, (Feb. 10, 1783,) in which he ſtyles himfelf one of his greateſt admirers, and by the gift of a gold fnuff-box fet with diamonds. When he had become King, he was equally gracious and friendly in returning his thanks for the engraved ſcore. (*Palamède,* t. vii. pp. 179—181.)

* Fétis.—[It appears, however, that Philidor had received the fame honour twenty-one years before. "À la première repréſentation du *Sorcier*, le parterre, tranſporté d' admiration, demanda les auteurs, ce

This detail of the profeſſional labour performed
by Philidor, from 1775 to 1785, while a third of
each year was ſpent with the London Cheſs-Club,
preſents the piƈture of a muſician, ſtill devoted to
his art, who may have yielded ſomething to the
demands of advancing years and of threatening
infirmity—ſomething, perhaps, to the capricious
exaƈtions of a poetic conſtitution—when enabled
to do ſo by the increaſe of his income from another
ſource, but who never ceaſed to do full juſtice to his
profeſſion, his family, or himſelf.*   No loſs of re-

---

qui n'était pas encore arrivé à la *Comédie-Italienne.* Philidor eut cela
de commun avec Voltaire, qui, le premier, avait reçu cet hommage au
Théâtre-Français, à l'occaſion de *Mérope.*" (Caſtil-Blaze, *De l'Opéra,* t.
i. p. 17.)]

* Philidor in his laſt years ſuffered from gout. From a paltry
anecdote of Grimm's—whoſe malicious goſſip ſpared nobody—I ſhould
infer, that before 1785 Philidor's conſtitution had begun to be ſhaken.
(*Correſpondance,* t. iii. p. 362.)—That Philidor could no more obey
Dr. Johnſon's preſcription to "work doggedly," without regard to
mood or condition, than others, who produce by genial inſpiration
and not by talent alone—(juſt as Milton could compoſe only in winter, and Goethe could reduce to writing only what he had never ſpoken
of to another)—appears from an early letter of his to Favart, written
at a period (1763) when his ſucceſs ſhould have put him in the beſt of
ſpirits.—"Monſieur, Depuis quinze jours, que j'ai votre poëme entre
les mains, j'ai voulu eſſayer pluſieurs fois y travailler, mais j'ai trop
d'humeur et de chagrin pour avoir la tête tranquille. En conſéquence,
il ne m'eſt pas poſſible de me charger d'aucun ouvrage de théâtre.
. . . . Je ne puis m'accoutumer à une ſuite conſtante de décourage-
ment."

putation or of popularity had given him caufe to abandon his art in difguft. And yet, M. Fétis affures us, that *Thémiftocle* was Philidor's laft opera; that after the compofition of this piece, he ceafed to work for the ftage; and that he gave himfelf up, without referve or reftraint, to his paffion for Chefs.—fpending the greater part of every day at the *Cafe de la Régence.* Were the facts really as ftated by M. Fétis, they would by no means juftify the harfh inference, which he muft have expected his readers to draw from them. In his ignorance of Philidor's engagement with the London Club, he fuppofes him to have fpent the whole of every year from 1779 to 1795 at Paris; and when he fays, that Philidor abandoned mufic and fpent his time in playing Chefs, he means to charge him with leaving his family to comparative deftitution for the fake of a piece of felf-indulgence, which under fuch circumftances would be abfolutely criminal. Philidor *might* have played Chefs all day at *La Régence* without fo entirely betraying the interefts of his family. His falary from the London Club, his penfion from the King, and his perquifites as a compofer of operas always on the ftage, would have furnifhed them with refources—if not abundant—yet adequate perhaps to their neceffities. M. Fétis, however, is fomewhat miftaken, even in his facts: Philidor did *not* ceafe, in 1785, to labour as a mufi-

cian, nor even to write for the ſtage. We have
Philidor's own authority, in Twiſs's anecdotes, that
in 1787 he compoſed *La belle Eſclave,* and in 1789
Le Mari comme il les faudrait tous.* By his corre-
ſpondence it appears, that in 1789 he alſo produced
a very elaborate compoſition for ſome celebration of
the recovery of George III. from his firſt attack of
inſanity; and that in 1790 he was preparing to
bring out, in London, a *Te Deum.*† It is by no
means likely, that we have an abſolutely complete
account of *all* Philidor did as a compoſer, eſpecially
during the later period of his life, when he was leſs
prominently before the public, than he had been in
his youth; but we have fortunately enough to vin-

---

* M. Fétis himſelf mentions *La belle Eſclave* among the works of
Philidor, but he avows himſelf unable to give the date.

† It appears from Philidor's letters, that the compoſition in queſtion
was an Ode in Engliſh, ſet to muſic at the requeſt of Gallini, Director
of the London Opera-houſe. The lively profeſſional ſpirit, with
which he expreſſed himſelf to his wife, while working at this taſk in
old age, was worthy of his beſt years : " J'avance dans mon ouvrage,
et je ſuis très content de mes idées. Je n'ai rien négligé, et j'oſe dire,
que j'ai fait l'impoſſible pour me mettre en peu de temps au fait de la
proſodie et de l'accent de la langue anglaiſe. J'eſpère réuſſir, et je compte
que je reviendrai avec tous mes brouillons de la totalité de mon ouvrage.
*J'ai la plus grande envie de prouver que la viéilleſſe ne m'a pas encore
éteint le génie.*"—[I now think it probable, that the *Te Deum* may
have been an old compoſition—the ſame which is mentioned in the
Mercure Français for June, 1773, (p. 145,) as having been performed
at the *Concert Spirituel* of that ſeaſon.]

dicate him from the charge of even a venial dere-
liction of his duty. If the written record of his
works had really ended abruptly—as it does with
Fétis—in 1785, we fhould ftill feel the moft entire
affurance, that more had ftill been done—even until
the laft days of his life—by a mufician, who, like
Gluck, had grown higher in his profeffional afpirations as he had advanced in years, and whofe felf-
facrificing devotion to his family—the trait of character, which is efpecially treafured up in facred
remembrance by his defcendants—muft have always
fupplied him with motives for continually exerting
his powers as a compofer.*

---

* The fuppofition is, befides, all but abfurd, that fuch a father of a
family—or even any man of found mind, *without* a family—fhould
play Chefs *temperately* up to the age of fifty-five, and then fuddenly
become a Chefs-*maniac*, deaf to all confiderations of duty and propriety.

CHAPTER VI.

FRENCH REVOLUTION—PHILIDOR'S LAST VISIT TO
ENGLAND—DEATH AND CHARACTER.

EANWHILE the whirlpool of the
Revolution was beginning to fet in
motion thofe fatal circles, which were
deftined to involve, with the reft, the
feelings and interefts of the harmlefs Chefs-player,
now compaffed about with years and infirmity. It
is no difcredit to Philidor, that he was, as his de-
fcendant has called him, "a man of *Eighty-Nine*"*—
that he fympathized warmly with the movement for
the abolition of the old privileges and abufes, and

---

* It was "an hard faying" of the great New-England Judge,
" *Th'oph Parfons*," (fo called,) in reference to the men of his own
time and place, who fympathized with the firft promifes of the French
Revolution—"The man, who is *not* a Democrat at twenty, is a *knave*;
the man, who *is* a Democrat at forty, is a *fool*."—Artifts and Poets
are always under twenty. Philidor found himfelf in company with,
not only artifts and poets, philofophers and *favants*, but alfo with the
beft of the clergy, the untitled rural *curés*.

for the fubftitution of a limited monarchy in place
of a defpotifm, which had now become even more
contemptible than onerous. His fentiments are free-
ly expreffed in the laft letters of his we have—thofe
of 1790. By that time the Revolution, which had
hitherto prefented nothing but "a pleafant exercife
of hope and joy" to minds like his, had, as he fuppofed, fairly completed its courfe—France was in
poffeffion of a good king as the head and centre of
free inftitutions, and Philidor afked and wifhed for
nothing more. He predicts in February, that before the month of July his country would have
fecured the admiring refpect of the univerfe—law-
fuits would be few or none, taxes would be reduced
at leaft a third, and yet the intereft of the public
debt would be honeftly paid. Nay, the very character of the nation would henceforth be changed;
the education of the young would be quite other
than it had been; people—*French* people—would
meet to converfe gravely and on grave fubjects, and
no longer wafte time in frivolity and nonfenfe. He
regrets, that, while he himfelf feels nothing but un-
utterable joy and patriotic pride, his firft-born, our
André, fhould not more fully fympathize with him;
he is delighted, however, that his fons have been
enrolled in the National Guard, and hopes that
"his young foldiers" will do their duty. He alludes
to Lafayette in terms to fatisfy even a grateful

American, and fuggefts the propriety of raifing an altar to the Bifhop of Autun, better known as the faintly Charles Maurice Talleyrand. In fhort, thefe perfectly honeft and homely utterances of Philidor to his wife, more than any high-wrought literary effort, make real to us the inconceivable fafcination exerted upon the beft men—men "who were ftrong in love"—by this firft apparition of "Her that rofe upon the banks of Seine," before the civic wreath, wherewith fhe bound her temples, had betrayed "the breathings of her dragon creft."*

Philidor was flow to believe that the character of ferocity, which the movement foon began to

---

* O pleafant exercife of hope and joy!
For mighty the Auxiliars, which then ftood
Upon our fide, we who were ftrong in love.
            WORDSWORTH—*French Revolution.*

    Who rifes on the banks of Seine,
And binds her temples with the civic wreath?
What joy to read the promife of her mien!
How fweet to reft her wide-fpread wings beneath!
        *   *   *   *
But fhe through many a change of form hath gone,
And ftands amidft you now an armed creature,
Whofe panoply is not a thing put on,
But the live fcales of a portentous nature;
That, having wrought its way from birth to birth,
Stalks round—abhorred by Heaven, a terror to the Earth!
    I marked the breathings of her dragon creft—
                WORDSWORTH—*Ode.*

exhibit, was anything more than accidental and tranfient. He had had fome experience of popular excitements in England—Lord George Gordon's Mob had filled London with much braying and fome burning during one of his London feafons— and he looked for nothing worfe from the wolfifh gang of Marat: he was prepared for the demolition of a prifon and a palace or two, but not for the cry of "*A la lanterne!*"—"*Parbleu, ma chère!* (he would fay to his wife) they really mean to fet Paris on fire by the four corners—give me my cane, and let me go and fee." But it is evident, that Philidor faw and heard, at laft, a good deal more than he liked. For towards the clofe of the year 1792—that is, after the blood of the September maffacres had tainted the air of France—without waiting, as had been his wont to do, for the month of February to come, he made his way to England. He obtained a paffport from the ruling authority of the time; and there is impreffive evidence, that he never ranked himfelf with the enemies even of the revolutionary government of his country; but I have no doubt it was a wholefome fear of *another* "celebrated" *La Régence* player, and not the declaration of war by England after the execution of Louis, that prevented any attempt to return home during the years 1793 and 1794 :—Maximilian Robefpierre might have feen in him, not the harmlefs Chefs-player, but the penfioner of two Kings and the favourite of a fugitive pretender to the crown.* At all events, it muft have been a matter of congratulation to his family, that during the Reign of Terror Philidor was not merely in fafety, but alfo in the midft of the friends of twenty years. In all other refpects, indeed, his fituation was neceffarily fuch as to prey conftantly upon his fpirits, and to weaken ftill more his enfeebled health.† He bore up under his afflictions, however, as he might, and frequented the Club as in happier days. He ftill proved at the board, that neither age nor difeafe had taken aught

---

* I think André Philidor good authority for his father's going to England before his ufual time, and for his having obtained a paffport —but not from the *Committee of Public Safety*, for that body, as known to hiftory, was not conftituted until April 6th, 1793. The inference from his going earlier than ufual is not only fair and natural, but is alfo fupported by current tradition, as given in Fétis and the *Palamède*. André makes the war the caufe of his father's not attempting to return; but Philidor had gone to and fro, without let or hinderance, during three previous wars.—The *Palamède* and Mr. Walker preferve the tradition, that Robefpierre was a Chefs-player and a regular frequenter of the *Café de la Régence*.—Monsieur (afterwards Louis XVIII.) was a member of the Paris Chefs-Club, and a fubfcriber to the *Analyfe* of 1777. I have fomewhere read, that he was alfo, on one occafion, an adverfary of Philidor's in a blindfold match, and that he tried in vain to difconcert him by making a falfe move.

† He had accounted even his annual voluntary feparation from his family an exile—"Enfin, voilà dejà un mois paffé de mon *exil*; je voudrais être au bout de mes engagements, pour vivre avec toi." (*Letter*, Feb. 20th, 1788.)

from the ftrength of his play, and he ftill ventured, without danger, upon what Diderot had called the "perilous eſſay" of his blindfold matches. So late as February and March, 1794, when ſixty-eight years old, the Turkiſh ambaſſador ſaw him, with admiration, conduct, the firſt time two, the ſecond three, games at once—with the ſlight relief, which he ſometimes allowed himſelf in later years, of having one of the three boards under his own eye.*

At length the Reign of Terror had paſſed away— the laſt *fournée* of Fouquier-Tinville had fed the

---

* The preſence of the Turkiſh ambaſſador, at theſe matches, appears to have emboldened his Interpreter—ſome lying Greek, I preſume—to circulate the ſtory, *after Philidor's death*, that, immediately ſubſequent to his laſt exhibition, in 1795, the Turk had invited him to his houſe, and, after having beaten him in ſix conſecutive games, informed him, that there were ſeveral players in Conſtantinople, from whom he himſelf had to accept the Rook. I have no doubt of the falſehood; yet the ſtory *might* be true, without damage to Philidor's reputation:—the pieces were ſtrange and not eaſily diſtinguiſhable; and the game itſelf was not the European game of Cheſs—inaſmuch, *e.g.*, as the *Queen* had the move of the *Knight*. (Twiſs's *Miſcellanies*, vol. ii. pp. 112–14.) Mr. Walker, while juſtly exploding this ſilly ſtory, is a little unjuſt to Twiſs; but Silberſchmidt (*Lehrbuch*, p. 301) is perfectly glorious in his attempt to *outgreek* the genuine ſon of " *Græcia mendax*."—It was in like manner reported, (Twiſs, *Cheſs*, vol. i. p. 188,) that Philidor had been beaten by Kempelen's Automaton, in 1783—another falſehood, which was ſtill quite true; for Philidor, to favour the good baron's intereſts, played *alla Ganapierde*—he tried to get beaten and could not. He told André, who was with him at the time, that he had never played ſo fatiguing a game.

guillotine; and, by the opening of the year 1795, there was good profpect of a ftate of things, in which a quiet old man might reafonably hope for a natural death. To return to Paris, to breathe his laft in the bofom of his family, was the one object, on which all the afpirations and all the efforts of Philidor were now concentred. But when his friends at home made application, at the proper office of the new government, for the neceffary fafe-conduct, they found that Philidor was regarded as an *émigré* —a clafs held in peculiar abhorrence for their avowed fympathy, or perfonal co-operation, with the enemies and invaders of France. It was neceffary to collect teftimony, and to multiply applications to various Committees, in order to remove, if poffible, the obftacle created by this fatal fufpicion. Philidor, in the meanwhile, aware, it appears, of nothing but that his application was going through fome not unufual procefs of official routine, ftill kept up heart and hope, and actually gave exhibitions at the Club in February and May. At length, however, either becaufe he felt himfelf finking, or more probably becaufe he was in immediate expectation of receiving his paffport, he announced by advertifement, that "by particular defire, and pofitively for the very laft time, he would play, on Saturday, the 20th of June, at two o'clock precifely, three games at once againft three good Chefs-players, two of them

without feeing either board, and the third on look-
ing over the table." Mr. Atwood, the celebrated
mathematician, was one of thofe players, and recorded the game in which he took part. The
prefence of Philidor is traced at the Club for a few
days longer. On the 29th of June he played two
games with Mr. Atwood at the odds of the Pawn
and Two Moves, of which he loft one. Both of
thefe games—with a reverent regard, no doubt, for
the laft efforts of the great mafter—were recorded
by Mr. Atwood, and were printed from his manu-
fcripts by Mr. Walker in 1835 for the firft time.
Philidor never vifited the Club again. He was now
made aware, that his paffport had been refufed, and
that he was on the lift of "fufpected characters,"
or "perfons who had been denounced by a Committee of French Informers." This fudden extinc-
tion of his one cherifhed hope, under circumftances
to fhut out, for him, all profpect of any change for
the better, proved to be more than he could bear.
"From this moment (in the words of the Obituary)
he became the martyr of grief—his philofophy for-
fook him—his tears were inceffant—and he funk
into the grave." He died on Monday, the 24th of
Auguft, 1795.* The fame affectionate notice gives

* It was a diftreffing circumftance, connected with Philidor's death,
that the information, which reduced him to defpair and made him an
unrefifting victim to his habitual infirmity, (the gout,) proved to be in

us the information, that "for the laft two months, Philidor had been kept alive merely by art, and the kind attentions of an old and worthy friend. To the laft moment of his exiftence, he enjoyed, though near feventy years of age, a ftrong retentive memory,

---

fo far unfounded, that his family finally fucceeded in procuring the fafe-conduct for him, juft in time to learn, that it had come too late.— It is fingular, that fo many dates fhould have been affigned to the death of Philidor. The *European Magazine, e.g.*, gives the 28th of Auguft; La Bourdonnais, (in his *Palamède* biography,) the 29th; Fétis, (after Choron and Fayolle, I fuppofe,) the 30th; and the *Gentleman's Magazine*—nay, André Philidor himfelf—the 31ft. Several of thefe authorities kindly allow Philidor a day or two for reading his own Obituary before taking his departure. La Bourdonnais fhould have been correct, for he had Walker's *Biographical Sketch* before his eyes; but, unhappily, his author had introduced the Obituary by faying: "On Saturday, Auguft 29th, the *public were informed* of the death of this unrivalled Chefs-player"—and the lazy tranflator, conceiving he had got his date already, fpared himfelf the trouble of reading any farther. The notice in the *European Magazine* contains only three or four lines; it is ten years out in Philidor's age; and is evidently, therefore, the work of one who *knew* as little as he *cared* about the matter. The only real authority—and it is perfectly fatisfactory—is the Obituary, which appeared in the London newfpapers, on Saturday, Auguft 29th. None of thofe papers are within my reach; but Twifs, whom I follow, (*Mifcellanies*, vol. ii. p. 110,) furnifhes good proof, that he had the original newfpaper document before his eyes, and that he copied it accurately, viz., he gives the day of the *week*, as well as the day of the *month*, of *both dates*—that of Philidor's death, and that of the newfpaper, which contained the Obituary. One French author, the Comte de Bafterot, (in his very interefting *Traité élémentaire*, p. 48,) and the always accurate German *Schachzeitung*, (vol. ii. p. 36,) give the true date.

which long rendered him remarkable in the circle of his acquaintances; and he was a man of thofe meek qualities, that rendered him not lefs efteemed as a companion, than admired for his extraordinary fkill."*

The tribute thus paid to the memory of Philidor was evidently the expreffion of fincere refpeĉt and regret. The Club, of which he had been for more than twenty years a member, fufpended their meetings for fome time after his death, "as a mark of refpeĉt to the immortal name of Philidor." So we are informed by Mr. Walker.† I wifh he had not added, that "it was difgraceful to them, that no funeral tablet was ereĉted, to point out the place of his reft." I wifh he had not charged "the great, the noble, the wealthy" patrons of Philidor with fuffering him to die, "almoft literally in a garret, deprived of thofe comforts, which foothe down the afperities of utter deftitution."‡ Mr. Walker is,

---

* In this paragraph I have compared and reconciled, as well as I could, André Philidor's ftatement and the Obituary in Twifs's *Mifcellanies*, vol. ii. pp. 110–12. From the letters of Mme George Sand's father, in her *Mémoires*, it appears that André had fome influence with the revolutionary authorities, even during the Reign of Terror. It is Twifs (*ut fuprà*) that gives Philidor's laft advertifement.—Mr. Atwood's MS. notes were publifhed in Mr. Walker's "*Seleĉtion of Games aĉtually played by Philidor:*" London, 1835.

† "*Seleĉtion of Games,*" p. 61.

‡ "*Chefs without the board,*" in Walker's *Chefs and Chefs-players*, p. 127. (From *Frafer's Magazine* for March, 1840.)

indeed, entitled—by his uniform zeal for the glory
of Philidor, and by his own noble conduct in the
cafe of La Bourdonnais*—to vifit with indignant
cenfure any real neglect of the dying mafter by the
Englifh Club; but I am bound to fay, in juftice to
an honourable affociation of gentlemen, that I believe the charge of fuch neglect to be entirely unfounded. The charge is made by Mr. Walker
alone, and is bafed folely (fo far as appears) upon
oral tradition† collected by himfelf. The facts fo
afcertained amount to precifely three more than *he*

---

* La Bourdonnais came to London, in the laft ftages of a dropfy,
late in November, 1840. It was prefently afcertained, that he was
on the point of being ejected from the garret, to which he had been
compelled to retreat. A Committee of Englifh Chefs-players, of whom
Mr. Walker was one, fubfcribed a hundred pounds, within half an
hour, for the relief of the fuffering ftranger. They removed him to
comfortable lodgings; procured medical affiftance; and beftowed every
kind of attention upon him until his death. They attended the funeral
in a body, and placed over his grave a ftone, with the infcription—
Louis-Charles de LA BOURDONNAIS, *the celebrated Chefs-player,*
died December 13*th,* 1840, *aged* 43. Nor did they paufe in their noble
work, until they had raifed a large fum for Madame La Bourdonnais
herfelf. It is a pleafure to renew the record of fuch acts as thefe.

† How uncertain any Chefs-*tradition* is may be inferred from that
of the *Café de la Régence,* on which M. Fétis relied, and by which
he was mifled. I muft add, that the Englifh tradition, on which Mr.
Walker relies, is ftill more fufpicious, becaufe it betrays a partifan
animus. It probably came to him through fome Chefs-player, whofe
focial pofition or political opinions led him either to invent facts, or to
interpret harmlefs real facts, to the injury of a Club compofed, to a
great extent, of "the great, the noble, and the wealthy."

had learned, as well as we, from the newfpaper
Obituary; and it is curious to obferve, how completely this enthufiaftic writer has magnified the
real weight of thefe facts—for fuch readers, efpecially, as have never learned to make allowance for
the *furor irlandefe**—by the redundant vehemence
of the figurative language, in which he envelopes
them. They *appear* to prove, that the gentlemen of
the Club left Philidor to die in a garret; that the
"old and worthy friend," who faved him from dying
abfolutely alone, "fupported" him, with no affiftance
from them; and that they took no thought for his
funeral, any more than for his monument. M. St.
Amant, accordingly, clothing the impreffion he had
thus received in a vefture as flowery as his author's,
holds up to his countrymen the wretched picture
of Philidor's "pauper-like condition," and of his
"death in a garret."† But Mr. Walker *really* fays

---

* When the Italians adopted the term *furor francefe* to denote a
model madnefs, they probably had not extended their obfervations beyond the continent.

† That is, Mr. Walker fpeaks of "the afperities of utter deftitution" in fuch exciting terms, that M. St. Amant underftands this
quite unappropriated "utter deftitution" to be the "état voifin de la
pauvreté" of Philidor in particular; and, the pathos of the "*almoft*
literally in a garret" being entirely too overwhelming to permit the
tender-hearted Frenchman to recognife the exiftence of the trifling
limitary particle, he fpeaks of the Englifh Committee, in the cafe of
La Bourdonnais, as "recollecting [*quite* literally] the garret of Philidor." (*Palamède-St. Amant*, t. i. pp. 16, 17.)

only that Philidor "died *almoſt* literally in a garret"
—which, being interpreted, clearly means, that
Philidor did *not* die in a garret at all.*   Of the remaining two traditionary facts, Mr. Walker appears
not to have reflected, that the one completely neu-
tralizes the other:—the fact, that the members of
the Club took immediate cognizance of the death
of their beloved maſter, by a very unuſual act of
official mourning, makes it utterly prepoſterous to
infer from the fact of their failing to erect a tablet
to his memory, that they had taken no thought of
his ſufferings or his wants on his death-bed.   The
aſſertion, that the dying old man was "chiefly indebted for *ſupport* to the aſſiduities of one kind
friend," is a very careleſs deviation from the lan-

---

* It is not pretended, that Philidor—after having occupied better
lodgings until his ſickneſs—was then obliged (and was ſuffered by his
Engliſh friends) to retire to his "almoſt a garret," and that there was
therefore the ſame reaſon for removing him, as exiſted in the caſe of
poor La Bourdonnais.   For all that appears, he died in the ſame modeſt
quarters, which he had choſen to live in during his laſt reſidence in
London.   If they were leſs expenſive, than he had been wont to oc-
cupy, it was undoubtedly becauſe the anxious circumſtances, under
which he was now living there, made every kind of economy both
neceſſary and becoming.   He was to meet the expenſe, not of a four
months', but of an indefinitely long, reſidence in a foreign city.   His
penſion was gone—probably his theatrical perquiſites, beſides.   His
family would need anything he could poſſibly economize from his
London ſalary and other earnings.   Self-denial and economy of this
kind might be carried far, without involving any ſuch diſtreſs, as
would attract or require the attention of his friends.

guage of the Obituary :—Philidor was " *kept alive*
for the laſt two months merely by *art*, and by the
kind attentions of an old and worthy friend ;" but
there is nothing whatever in *theſe* words to juſtify
what appears to be Mr. Walker's conſtruction, that
the kind friend *ſupported the expenſe* of what was
done for Philidor, "to keep him alive," either by
medical art or otherwiſe.

If, therefore, the charges of Mr. Walker againſt
the Engliſh Club are far from being ſuſtained even
by the traditionary facts, which he himſelf adduces,
ſtill leſs able are they to ſtand their ground againſt
the ſtrong preſumptive evidence, that can be brought
in conflict with them.   For twenty years, the gentlemen of the Club had ſhown the moſt delicate
and ſyſtematic attention to the pecuniary intereſts
and perſonal comforts of Philidor.   While their
number had been decreaſing, they had kept up his
ſalary.   They had anticipated his wants by advancing their ſubſcriptions.*   They had arranged and

---

* We know, (*Letter*, February, 1790,) that on one occaſion, certainly—and probably often or always—Count Brühl and General Conway paid Philidor their quota (a large proportion, too) of his ſalary,
immediately on his arrival in England, and long before the ſubſcription
was opened in the Club.—[The Rev. Mr. Pruen's *Introduction to the
Hiſtory and Study of Cheſs* (p. 30) confirms what I have already ſaid,
(*antè*, p. 78,) that Philidor had the opportunity (evidently with the
ſanction and encouragement of the Club) to earn a good deal by playing as an inſtructor.   His ſtake (underſtood to be a tuition-fee) was a
crown a game.]

patronifed frequent blindfold exhibitions in order to increafe his income. Count Brühl had reduced his London expenfes a full half, by making him a daily gueft at his table—a ftep, which he would not have reforted to, if his feeling towards him had not come to be that of fincere perfonal friendfhip. Such appears to have been the habitual conduct of the members of the Club towards Philidor up to the laft day of his prefence among them; and we have feen how entirely confiftent with fuch conduct was their official action immediately after his death. Is it, then, within the bounds of poffible belief, that for folely and precifely the two months, which elapfed between thefe two dates, thefe fame kind, confiderate, and attentive friends fhould have become unkind, inconfiderate, and inattentive to the fame old man, under circumftances to make the withholding of any poffible kindnefs, confideratenefs, and attention mere barbarity ?*

---

* Another confideration, which has great weight with me, I do not introduce into the text, becaufe it is merely negative—viz., the papers of André Philidor do not betray the flighteft knowledge of any fuch neglect of his father. Yet, as the family immediately received fuch details of Philidor's laft illnefs, as could not have been learned from the Obituary, it is reafonable to fuppofe, that the communication came from one, who muft alfo have known—if the fact were really fo—that "one old friend" had been compelled to bear every expenfe, and perform every kind office, required by the occafion, becaufe thofe, who had fo long profeffed to be the friends of the great Chefs-player,

For my own part, I believe nothing of the kind. I do not entertain the flighteft doubt, that the "old and worthy friend" was in communication with the gentlemen of the Club, and that he was enabléd to perform his pious office, even to the laft rites of fepulture, by means, which they fupplied. If the Obituary paffes over what *they* did, to record the perfonal devotion of that one old friend, it is probably becaufe the Obituary itfelf was prepared by one of their own number. It is true, his former affociates fet up no tablet to his memory*—an omif-

---

had barbaroufly deferted him. If the informant were cognizant of fuch a faĉt, he could hardly have forborne to difclofe it, fo far, at leaft, as was neceffary, in order to do full juftice to the "old friend;" the impreffion thus left in the family could not have been forgotten, nor would it have been fuppreffed by the fon in preparing a biography of his father.—The filence of Twifs is alfo of fome weight. He had had little to do with Philidor, it is true, after 1787; but if he was fond enough of malicious goffip to record the viĉtories of the Turkifh ambaffador, he could hardly have failed to know or preferve fo bad a trait of charaĉter as the unfeeling conduĉt of the Englifh Club.

* That is to fay, I *accept* it as true, on Mr. Walker's mere word, rather than to be always difputing him, or impertinently calling upon him to prove a negative. But what if Mr. Walker himfelf has thought better of his denying the exiftence of a monument? He did, indeed, make that denial, in 1835, in fo many words; but, in 1840, he merely fays, "Philidor paffed from life in fuch obfcurity, that I have never yet been able to difcover the fpot where he was buried." (*Chefs and Chefs-players*, p. 127.) If this pofition be really a fubftitute for the earlier one, the denial of the monument is, of courfe, given up; for Mr. Walker's inability to find the cemetery, in which Philidor was

fion not regretted by one alone of Philidor's biographers; but the inference, that thofe, who failed
to do all they might have done *after* his death, had
failed to do anything for him while dying, is war-
ranted neither by found reafon nor by actual experience:—it has often happened, that where a fincere feeling of regret, and even of gratitude, has
prompted the tribute of an act of piety like this,
the execution of the purpofe falls through from
caufes, that cannot fairly be faid to involve either
reproach or difgrace.

The connection of Philidor with the Englifh
Club is without a parallel in the hiftory of Chefs:
it exhibits a picture of Chefs-talent and of perfonal
merit fo perfectly appreciated and fo honourably rewarded, as to reflect equal credit upon the noble
patrons and upon the fubject of their patronage.
For the honour of human nature, fuch a picture
fhould not wantonly be marred or defaced. I have
not, therefore, thought it at all out of place to
fubject to the fevereft teft of critical examination
the traditionary charge, which would make the life

---

buried, would as well prove that he had no grave, as that his grave
had no ftone, and that he did not die at all, as that he died in obfcurity.
We do not ufually conceive of that departure as an obfcure one, which
is immediately followed by the protracted adjournment of a fociety of
diftinguifhed men, and to the announcement of which half a column
is devoted in the leading weekly newfpapers.

of Philidor to have clofed under circumftances to embitter tenfold the chalice, which he was doomed to drink in folitude and in exile, to the endlefs difgrace of men, for whom otherwife we could entertain no other fentiments, than thofe of peculiar refpeĉt and gratitude.   I wifh I might hope, that every reader is as fully fatisfied as I am, that the charge is a calumny.*

It may feem quite unneceffary, after prefenting fo much of biographical detail, that fpeaks for itfelf, to keep the hand ftill upon the tablet, in an attempt to delineate the charaĉter of Philidor.   Where, however, the biographer has been labouring to reftore to all its rights a name, to which fome injuftice has been done, he may be indulged, by the good-natured reader, in a few words more, than what is merely enough.   Philidor has too long been an objeĉt of living intereft to the Chefs-player alone, and to him folely as a Chefs-player.   But to me no part of my theme has been more attraĉtive, than that which invited me to fearch carefully into all the evidences of what my hero afpired to do, and what he accom-

---

* In a letter received after the preceding fheet had been printed, Mr. Lewis (the eminent Englifh Chefs-author and player) kindly anfwered fome inquiries of mine, by faying : " Who ' the old and worthy friend' was, I know not.   I always underftood from Sarratt, that a Mr. Crawford, a very rich man, patronifed Philidor, taking a leffon— or being *fuppofed* to take a leffon—daily, and giving him *carte blanche* to dinner, whenever it fuited him."

plifhed, as a Muſician.   It has been matter of ſerious
gratification to me to be able to fhow, that the moſt
celebrated of all Chefs-players treated the game as a
game, and not as a profeſſion ; and that he referved
all the aⅽtivity of the beſt years of his life for his
noble Art.   For this Philidor would deferve our re-
ſpeⅽt, even if his honourable induſtry had procured
him nothing more than his daily bread—if it had
produced no works of more than temporary intereſt—if it had won him no place among thoſe, whoſe
names the world " does not willingly let die."   But
ſuch was not the caſe.   The name of Philidor muſt
live, in the Hiſtory of Muſic, even if all his works
muſt periſh.   All the aψthors of French muſical hiſtory, from La Borde, through Caſtil-Blaze and Fétis,
down to Poiſot, unite in declaring, that Philidor ſus-
tained the leading part in the work of founding the
moſt thoroughly national of all his country's muſical
entertainments, the *Opéra-Comique.**   Nor can the
reform of the ſerious opera ever be mentioned, without doing Philidor the juſtice of having been the firſt
and only compoſer, that achieved a ſucceſs, which

---

* Fétis ſays, (*Curioſités*, p. 358,) in reference to Philidor's coöpe-
ration with Monfigny in creating the *Opéra-Comique*, "L'autre (Philidor) poſſédait plus de ſcience muſicale que tous ſes compatriotes."—
Caſtil-Blaze, (*De l'Opéra*, t. i. p. 33,)—after ſpeaking of the earlier
French compoſers—adds, "Si l'on excepte PHILIDOR et M. Goſſec,
aucun n'avait cette ſcience profonde, ce ſtyle grandioſe, qui comman-
dent l'admiration dans tous les pays."

could be perfected and made durable by no gentler agencies than the energetic genius, the iron will, and the terrific *bâton* of Gluck.

No compofer creates or reforms a department of the Lyric Drama by dint of mere talent and mufical fcience. Without, therefore, claiming for Philidor an equality with the five or fix Immortals of the art, it is fafe to affert, that he poffeffed Genius, and that too of a high order. We cannot, to be fure, appeal for the proof to the living utterances of the concert-room or the ftage. But we can produce witneffes, whofe competency cannot be called in queftion. Grétry, his contemporary, puts Philidor fide by fide even with Gluck himfelf, for " force of harmonic expreffion."* Fétis, at the fame time the Neftor and the Corypheus of living mufical critics, awards to the works of Philidor a peculiar ftamp of originality. And both of thefe high authorities afcribe to him a characteriftic mark of genius,—the difpofition and the capacity to invent new means of expreffion. One inftances his new orcheftral effects ; the other, original combinations of rhythm.†

---

* *Mémoires,* (1829,) t. i. p. 157. "Si les muficiens de nos jours étaient jugés par l'efprit qui caractérifait les anciens, l'on nommerait Gluck et Philidor, pour la force de l'expreffion harmonique."

† *Antè,* p. 47, and the foot-notes pp. 65–67. I add here the words of fome additional authorities. Fétis fays of *Thémiftocle,* much as he had faid of *Ernelinde,* " Cet ouvrage eft remarquable . . . par *la nouveauté des formes de l'inftrumentation.*"—The earlier opera-compofers

Nor is it the cafe, that French critics are thus loud in their teftimony, while all "the reft is filence." The German fchool, which may affuredly claim fuch richnefs of production as to tempt a difdain for what foreign fchools have brought forth, has recog-nifed the fingular merit of Philidor, in a fpirit of juft and dignified appreciation, that might well have been imitated by fome of his own countrymen. While Frenchmen have been found mean enough to charge one of the moft fingle-minded and honeft of men with fyftematic plagiarifm, the higheft German au-thorities have diftinctly avowed, that Philidor ftood by himfelf, a century ago, in working in the fpirit of their own later mafters; that not only are his fcores ftudied (as they deferved to be) by every young compofer, that would fee real mufic feparated from all that is trivial and temporary, but that remarkable evidence of fuch ftudy has been given by the clofe reproduction of fome of his beauties by a dramatic

---

(according to Caftil-Blaze and Fétis) had no *Finales* or larger combi-nations of voices: "Cependant PHILIDOR (Fétis, *La Mufique mife à la portée*, etc. p. 160) faifit l'occafion qui lui fut offerte dans *Tom Jones* pour faire un bon Quatuor."—Grétry (Letter in the *Mercure Fran-çais*, 1795) writes,—"Muficien profond, c'eft lui qui le premier fit entendre fur la fcène françaife les accens mélodieux des Italiens joints à la force de l'harmonie et du génie des Allemands . . . Philidor eft, je crois, l'inventeur des morceaux de mufique à plufieurs fujets où à plufieurs rhythmes contractans. Le duo de *Tom Jones*, '*Que les de-voirs que tu m'impofes*,' eft le chef-d'œuvre des morceaux de ce genre."

compofer of their own, who in original creative power ranks fecond to none.*

If the Operas of Philidor no longer form part of any current repertory, it is fimply becaufe an audience of the day demands to be fpoken to in the language and fpirit of the day, with the multiplied and novel appliances of the day. The orcheftra of Philidor, a ftartling and novel one for the old *Foire S. Laurent*, would appear thin and tame by the fide of the "flutes and trumpets" of the actual *Opéra-Comique*. But although the tide of fafhion, that fwept away all fecond-rate productions at once, had begun to fet in even before Philidor's death, fuch was the native charm of his lighter works, that they continued to flourifh on the ftage, as frefh as ever, fo late as the

---

* "Philidor won for himfelf a reputation, which—in the minds of fuch as really underftand the fubject—can never be loft; for his works are (to fay all in one word) full of *German* ftrength and folidity. In *Blaife* and his other operas, there lives a *German* fpirit; and it is for this reafon, that they have been the models of fome of *our* moft fuccefsful compofers. An *amalgam* with our Carl Maria von Weber is very diftinctly vifible in a duet of *Tom Jones* and one in *Der Freifchütz*, viz.: *Que les devoirs que tu m'impofes!* and *Halt! halt feft!* Place them fide by fide, and the fact will be demonftrated; the interval of more than half a century vanifhes, both for feeling and for fight. The operas of Philidor are given, and received with applaufe, in every part of Europe; and are induftrioufly ftudied by all fuch young compofers as make it their aim to cut loofe from every kind of *fing-fong* and *cling-clang*." (Schindler's *Univerfal Lexicon der Tonkunft*, Stuttgart, 1837.)

days of the Firft Napoleon.* Fétis, writing in 1841,
affirms, that *Le Maréchal Ferrant* had then been
produced in Paris more than two hundred times.†

But, of courfe, it is as a Chefs-player, that Philidor
holds a place among the privileged few, whofe claim
to be the *Primarii*—" the foremoft men of all the
world," in their refpective fpheres—has been fettled
by an action, on the part of their fellow-men, as au-
thoritative as it is indefinable—by a tacit admiffion
of fupremacy, a general and fpontaneous act of homage.   In his own day he ftood, in the opinion of
the actual Chefs-world, abfolutely alone.   Whatever
may have been the ftrength in play of the contemporary theorifts, Ercole del Rio, Ponziani, and Lolli,
it was proved only in a peculiar fchool and exhibited
on an unknown ftage : it had no effect, therefore,
out of the Peninfula, to fuggeft the flighteft doubt
of the fupremacy of Philidor.   There was nothing,
confequently, to hinder the conviction of Philidor's
unique pofition from paffing beyond the circle of
Chefs-players into the world without—from being

---

* *Antè*, p. 46.—See alfo Scudo, *Critique* etc. t. ii. p. 474.—When
La Bourdonnais, writing fo late as 1836, (*Biographie*,) fays, that all
of Philidor's operas were forgotten, he excepts *le Maréchal ferrant*.—
For a very interefting analyfis of the *Maréchal ferrant*, fee the article
of M. Pougin already referred to (*antè*, p. 84.)

† We have Lardin's authority for the fact, that the compofitions of
Philidor were ftill (1841) treated as models, and given out as fubjects
of ftudy, in the celebrated *Confervatoire* of Paris.

univerfally recognifed as a fixed and indifputable
dogma, an immutable tradition. As fuch it appears,
everywhere, among the received commonplaces of
works of literature and fcience. The name of Philidor ftands out, in the general opinion, as diftinctly
from other names, as does that of Newton. It has
acquired a facrednefs, that may have had its effect
upon the judgments of the Chefs-critics of a later
day. In France, La Bourdonnais and St. Amant
did but conform to the univerfal feeling, when they
habitually fpoke of Philidor as their " Mafter," " the
Great Mafter," "the Mafter of us all."* The very
able Englifh editor and critic of his book and of his
games, George Walker, has everywhere, and in the
moft emphatic terms, characterized Philidor as " the
greateft Chefs-player that ever lived—the founder of
a fchool, which has proved itfelf fecond to none—
the head of a dynafty, which has included a Carlier, a Bernard, a Defchapelles, a La Bourdonnais."
Nay, herein Mr. Walker does but echo the equally
decifive but calmer language of his illuftrious friend,

---

* It is true, that La Bourdonnais—after having called Philidor
(*Palamède*, t. i. p. 392) "le joueur le plus extraordinaire qui ait jamais
paru"—argued, in a converfation with the Chevalier de Barneville, that
he could have given Philidor the Pawn and Two Moves (*La Régence*,
1851, p. 118.) But, for La Bourdonnais's fake, it may be well to
recollect, that he was, perhaps, (as ufual,) merely joking, and that we
have the anecdote upon the authority of M. Méry.

Alexander M'Donnell himſelf.* Many of the fore-
moſt Cheſs-writers have not heſitated, either directly
or by implication, to expreſs the further opinion,
that he, who had certainly never met his equal, in
his own day, would have undoubtedly ſuſtained the
ſame unique poſition, were he to have found himſelf ſeated oppoſite to the adepts, whoſe names have,
ſince his day, ſhone with ſo bright a luſtre in the
Cheſs-empyrean.†

Of all Cheſs-writers, he who is confeſſedly the
firſt in our own day, and ſecond to none that have
ever been, has ſhared leſs than moſt others that awe
for the Great Shade, which may have influenced
the opinions and the expreſſions of La Bourdonnais
and St. Amant, of Walker and M'Donnell.   Herr
VON HEYDEBRAND UND DER LASA has ſcrutinized
ſuch monuments, as we have, of Philidor's practical ſkill, with the ſame "judicial compoſure," the
ſame abſolute fairneſs, that characterize his critique
of the *Analyſe*.   The reſult will be found in the
ſecond ſection of the Eſſay, with which he has

---

* "I am very anxious to ſee the Philidor MS. *Philidor is my favourite;* and I prize whatever remains of him." (Autograph Letter
to Mr. Walker, in my poſſeſſion.)

† I may cite, for example, a clever writer in the *Quarterly Review*
(No. CLXIX, June, 1849, p. 94): "At the riſk of being deemed
either old-faſhioned or ignorant, we muſt plead guilty to a concluſion
leſs flattering to modern profeſſors. We believe, on the evidence of
Philidor's recorded games, that on the whole he has had no ſuperior."

enriched this book of mine. If the reader fhould, at firft, find his enthufiafm difagreeably chilled by the abfence of thofe warm expreffions of admiration, with which others—fuch as George Walker and I—inveft all mention of our Chefs-hero, he will, in the end, be better fatisfied, that the received opinion refts on a fure bafis, when he hears fo cool a critic, fo high an authority, declare his judgment, that there was *no* given meafure of practical fkill, which Philidor, in his beft days, could not have made his own. Forever, therefore, let the Star of Philidor dwell apart. Let us accord to La Bourdonnais and to our own PAUL MORPHY the credit of having attained an actual height, in Chefs-fkill, that had never been attained before ; but let us, by no fuch recognition of later and contemporary greatnefs, detract aught from the confecrated fupremacy of Philidor.

No words are required to fhow what Philidor was as a man. With even fuch fcanty details as we have of his private life, we feel that we need nothing more. We read him like a fairly written book. The fun never fhone upon a human being more perfectly fimple, fingle-hearted, and open. He loved his art for itfelf. He therefore felt no jealoufy of Monfigny, no envy of Gluck. He could, with equal fincerity, mourn the departure of Rameau, and welcome the rifing ftar of Grétry. As his Englifh friends, after his death, dwelt upon what they had witneffed—his meeknefs and gentlenefs, his difintereftednefs and his probity; fo Grétry, with more perfect knowledge of what he had been at home, honoured him as a good hufband, a good father, a good friend. It would be hard to believe, that fuch a man could have adopted, as a companion to fuch virtues, the wicked and ferocious irreligion of his time. With no evidence to the contrary, it is reafonable to cherifh the belief, that he had never abandoned the faith and the impreffions of his earlieft training, in daily affociation, as it was, with the moft facred offices of religion; and that he was not without the confolations of religion at his death. And, therefore, if thofe, who delight to honour his memory, may not be able to read, on any fepulchral ftone, the "forlorn *Hic jacet*" of Philidor, they may at leaft waft after him a devout *Requiefcat in pace!*

PHILIDOR

AS

CHESS-AUTHOR AND CHESS-PLAYER

CONTRIBUTED TO

THE LIFE OF PHILIDOR

AS A SUPPLEMENT

BY

Tassilo von Heydebrand und der Lasa

Chamberlain and Legationary Councillor to the King of Pruffia
Envoy Extraordinary and Minifter Plenipotentiary of the King of
Pruffia at the Grand Ducal Court of Saxe-Weimar-Eifenach
Principal author of the *Handbuch des Schachfpiels*
and author of *Leitfaden für Schachfpieler*
Berliner Schacherinnerungen
and many Papers on
Chess.

The following Effay was written at Rio Janeiro, in the winter of 1858-59, during the author's refidence in that capital as *Chargé d'affaires* of the King of Pruffia. It was fent to me in the original German, for tranfla-tion, with the requeft, that I would add to it Notes of my own. If the reader knew, as well as I do, with what force and propriety Herr von der Lafa expreffes himfelf in our language, he would regret that the origi-nal had not been written in Englifh at once. He will, at any rate, think none the worfe of my tafte for limit-ing my Notes to a few references or illuftrations.

G. A.

PHILIDOR

AS CHESS-AUTHOR AND CHESS-PLAYER.

N the following Effay, which is offered as a Supplement to the *Life of* PHILIDOR, it is propofed to difcufs the merit, which the *Analyfe* may poffefs, as a work of Chefs-theory, and to attempt fome eftimate of the Chefs-fkill of its author, in comparifon—fo far, at leaft, as fuch comparifon is admiffible or practicable—with, that of later and contemporary players.

I.

PHILIDOR AS CHESS-AUTHOR.

HILIDOR was indebted for his world-wide celebrity, not folely to his fuperiority in actual play over thofe of his contemporaries, whom he met over the board, but alfo as well to his perfonal relations with many men of high rank and diftinction, as to the

wide circulation, which his *Analyſe* attained, as the com-
pendium of what was, in that age, known of Chefs-play,
outſide of Italy. Of all French Chefs-authors, Philidor
is the only one, whoſe work has made an epoch in the
hiſtory of the game. No other produ&tion, in all Chefs-
literature, has been ſo frequently reprinted, both in the
original French, and in moſt of the languages of modern
Europe. We recogniſe in it, at once, the produ&tion of
a comprehenſive mind, ſtill bearing marks of youthful
exuberance, but endowed with a rare talent for the clear
exhibition of its ideas. The work has been judged of
very differently by different critics. Thoſe who pay an
excluſive homage to a ſyſtem, identical with that of the
Analyſe, have certainly rated its value too high. Others
—Ponziani, for example—who have dire&ted their attention to the *openings,* with little or no reference to the
ſubſequent proſecution of the game, have as evidently
rated it too low. Philidor himſelf was full of confidence
in his own capacity and in the value of his treatiſe. In
the Preface to his firſt edition, he ſpeaks ſlightingly
enough of " *Le Calabrois*" and of Bertin—of the " big
volume" of Carrera, wherein the good prieſt affirms, that
the checkmate by Rook and Biſhop againſt Rook is a
forced one, without being able (Philidor intimates) to
give the moves—and of the artificial Poſitions, which
could not occur in a&tual play ſo often as once in a thou-
ſand years. His own principal obje&t (he continues) is
to deſerve commendation by a novelty, of which nobody
before him had ever thought or perhaps been capable,
namely, to teach, by means of entire games, the proper

mode of playing the Pawns. "The Pawns" (he fays) "are the *Soul* of Chefs;" and it is upon the good or bad playing of the Pawns, that the winning or the lofing of the game entirely depends. This rather petulant Introduction—wherein the author rejects, with mockery and farcafm, the doctrine, that a Pawn can become a fecond Queen (although at a later day he accepted it)—was quietly dropt in the edition of 1777, and replaced by a fhorter one.

Philidor's treatife embraced, in its firft edition of 1749, only nine games, with their variations. Of thefe games four are *Common*, viz.:—No. I. is the *King's Bifhop's Game;* No. II. the *Queen's Bifhop's Pawn's Defence* in the King's Bifhop's Game; No. III. *Philidor's Defence* in the King's Knight's Game; and No. IV. is the *Queen's Bifhop's Pawn's Game.* After thefe follow *Gambits*, viz., the *King's Gambit Proper;* the *Cunningham Gambit;* the *Bifhop's Gambit;* the *King's Gambit declined;* and then the *Queen's Gambit*—a game efpecially commended by Stamma, and which Philidor—with evident reference to this circumftance—calls the *Aleppo Gambit.* There is alfo thrown into the bargain, as it were, a certain checkmate with Rook and Bifhop againft Rook, which, however, although a model of clear and precife analyfis, does not entirely demonftrate the affertion of Carrera. The fpecimens of play, which Philidor furnifhed, in his firft edition, were defigned chiefly to give the Chefs-ftudent a clue to guide him fafely through the *middle* of the game. Few as they are in number, only the four firft, even of thefe, were looked upon by him, as calculated to illuftrate his fyftem. The ftudy of fuch a collection, therefore, muft be entirely infufficient for conveying a knowledge of the *openings*. For this reafon, the author, in his fecond edition (1777)—which repeats without change all the moves of the firft, with only here and there a modification of the notes—adds a few fhort openings, at the clofe. It is much to be regretted, that during the interval between his two editions, Philidor had not come to know the three great Mafters, who at that time were flourifhing in Modena. A meeting with Ercole del Rio, the moft celebrated of the three, would not only have produced games of peculiar intereft, as being contefts between the reprefentatives of two different fyftems, but would alfo naturally have exerted a powerful influence upon the aims and labours of theorifts on both fides of the Alps. But this great event the Chefs-world was not permitted to fee.

Philidor's edition of 1777 is, therefore, even in its additional matter, penetrated by the fame fpirit as the earlier one. The *Games*, with the inftructive *Notes* appended to them, ftill form the ftaple of the work. Thefe conftitute the expofition of a peculiar fyftem, the characteriftic features of which, contrafted with thofe of the Italian fchool, I have endeavoured to give, in an effay of fome length, contributed to the Berlin *Schachzeitung* for 1847 and 1848. It can hardly be poffible, that thefe model Games ever occurred in actual play : they were, undoubtedly, compofed by Philidor himfelf for his work. They are diftinctively characterized by the thoroughly confequent and fyftematic ftyle of their Pawn-play, and

by the manner in which they make ufe of the central
Pawns to fecure clofenefs of pofition. They cannot,
however, be faid to have been conftructed upon princi-
ples abfolutely new; they are, more properly, the off-
fpring of the prevailing theories of the day—theories that
were bafed far more upon the games of Lopez, (of whofe
work there had been feveral editions in French,) than
upon thofe of Greco, in which the fpirit of the Italian
fchool was decidedly preponderant. The little book of
the Englifhman Bertin (1735,) and Stamma's Openings
(1745,) do in fact belong to the fame fchool as the *Analyfe*: what Philidor did was to perfect and expound the
fyftem of that fchool. When we examine the work in
this light—taking into account alfo the youthful years of
the author in 1749—it is impoffible not to concede to
Philidor a precocious maftery of all the recondite fubti-
lities of the game, and an extraordinary gift of exhibiting his ideas in a clear and comprehenfive plan. The
mark which Philidor aimed at was high and worthy of
a great mafter. And yet he would hardly have ventured
upon the execution of the tafk he had propofed to himfelf, if he had been fully aware how wide a field was
really embraced by it—if he had not, like his contemporaries, reftricted his obfervation to the one-fided " Pawn
game" alone. Neverthelefs the *Analyfe*—even in the
fhape wherein it firft appeared, in 1749—abundantly
proves, that its author poffeffed a remarkable talent for
dealing with the fcience of the game. This is a gift,
which many other great players have not poffeffed. I
do not prove this by inftancing in the celebrated, but

weak, *Traité des Amateurs,* becaufe I do not confider
that work to have been produced by " great players," of
a clafs to compare with Philidor.   But La Bourdonnais
is a cafe in point.   Although endowed with the very
higheft order of genius for the practice of the game, he
has left behind him, in his theoretical work, only a very
middling fort of compilation.*   I may cite alfo Deschapelles, another Hero of the later age, from whom, as an
antagonift in play, La Bourdonnais acquired much of his
fkill.   That great player never gave himfelf the flighteft
trouble about the theory of the game; nay, he rated
Chefs-fcience fo low, that when a move propofed by himfelf, in one of the famous correfpondence-games with
Pefth, was objected to, on grounds of Chefs-theory, as
not the ftrongeft, he could think of no better way to decide the difference between Chefs-fcience and himfelf,
than to challenge the entire Committee to play out the
reft of the game with him, over the board, for a wager.
He immediately refigned his place in the Committee,
when they declined accepting this fingular *cartel.*

The *Analyfe* contains many propofitions, afferted by
Philidor with too much confidence in 1749, which, at
maturer years, he was not difpofed to maintain, and
therefore difcarded in his fecond edition.   The fact,
however, that he had once afferted fuch propofitions,
continued, even after he had withdrawn them, to affect
prejudicially his authority as a theorift.   To thefe in-

---

* " Le pauvre La Bourdonnais et fon pauvre livre !"   " Déteftable
compilation !" are fome of the flowers fcattered by M. le Viceroi St.
Amant upon the *Nouveau Traité* of his Sovereign.—Tr.

ftances of youthful rafhnefs belong the unfounded cenfure, which he pronounced, in 1749, upon the *King's
Knight's Game*, the favourite opening of the Italians,—
the Notes on the third move in the Second Game,
(*Queen's Bifhop's Pawn's Defence* in the King's Bifhop's
Game,) with the illuftrative Firft Back-game,—and the
Notes on the opening moves of the Fourth Game—
Notes, from which it might be inferred, that Philidor
(like Carrera, 1617, p. 74) held the opinion, that to
have the firft move was to win the game. On the other
hand, if we find thefe few untenable precepts in the
Analyfe, we alfo find Notes, which enunciate very ftrik-
ing general propofitions, and Games decided by moves
well thought through, and univerfally recognifed to be
the ftrongeft. At the fame time, there is no lack, either
in the openings, or in the fubfequent moves, of fuch
overfights, as we can account for, only by fuppofing,
that the author gave more attention to the general character and main tendency of the games, than to the ana-
lytical accuracy of each move. How otherwife—to cite
only one example—can we account for it, that Philidor
fhould play out, to the advantage of Black, the pofition
in which his Cunningham-Gambit game ftands after the
29th move of Black, in the Second Variation ?*

He had taken fides with Black, and therefore remarks,
(in reference to this Pofition, on which he beftows par-

---

* The Pofition is : WHITE—King at KR ; Rook at QB7 ; Bifhops
at K3 and QR4; Knight at KB; Pawns at Q4, QKt5, and QR3.
BLACK—King at KKt3 ; Rook at Q2 ; Bifhop at K3 ; Knight at K2;
Pawns at KR4, KKt4, K5, Q4, QKt2, and QR2.

ticular attention,) that White would lofe, juft as well, were he even to avoid the exchange of Rooks. Philidor purfues the game as follows :* (WHITE) 30. R : R, (BLACK) B : R ; and thereupon continues with 31. K Kt2, KRP on ; 32. QB KB2, K KR4 ; 33. KB Q†, B covers ; inftead of allowing White to make the decifive move, 31. *QKtP on.* 'Without ftirring the queftion, who was the author of this move, it is fufficient for my prefent purpofe to fay, that it is mentioned in Walker's edition of the *Analyfe*, 1832.†

But I will here repeat the earlier moves of this Gambit, in order to attach to them a few notes, and to invite

---

* It being obvioufly neceffary to fubftitute, for the "algebraic" notation employed by the author, one more familiar to Englifh and American Chefs-players, I have adopted fubftantially that which appears in the later publications of George Walker, partly becaufe three of the games, cited in the Effay, were copied from Walker's *Selection*, and partly becaufe I do myfelf prefer Walker's to any other form of defcriptive notation, as being the moft compendious reproduction of the real language of Chefs-players over the board. For the convenience of the printer, I have made the flight change of adopting from German Chefs-books a colon (:) as equal to "takes," and the dagger (†) for "checks" or "checking."—TR.

† Walker's note is, "You may now get a fine game, *e. g.*, 31. QKtP on, B QB3 ; 32. P : P, QKtP2 ; 33. KB : P, B QR ; 34. Kt Kt3, and ought to win." The move 31. QKtP on appears firft (fo far as I know) in Pratt's *Studies in Chefs*, 1810, vol. ii. p. 17, where it introduces a "Variation *by the Editor*." Herr von der Lafa, I fuppofe, does not confider the claim thus afferted to be put beyond all queftion, inafmuch as honeft Peter was certainly abfolutely incapable of inventing any ftrong move whatfoever, not to fay a ftronger move than one of Philidor's.—TR.

attention to a flip or two, which Philidor has made in
this part of the game alfo. 1. KP2, KP2; 2. KBP2,
P : P ; 3. KKt B3, KB K2; 4. B QB4, KB KR5†; 5.
KtP covers, P : P ; 6. Caftles, P : P† ; 7. K to corner.
Philidor gives to this variation of the Knight's Gambit,
as Stamma had done before him, (although Stamma continues with 7. . . . . QP2,) the name of " *Cunningham's
Gambit*." The earlier Englifh author, Bertin, however,
(whofe little book, now fo very rare, Philidor was acquainted with,) calls it merely *The Three Pawns Game*,
without attaching to it the name of any inventor. It
has, therefore, been affumed by fome writers, (as, for
example, by Cochrane, 1822, p. 357,) that Bertin himfelf was the real inventor of this bold game. On this
point, nothing can be affirmed with certainty, Philidor
proceeds thus : B KB3 ; 8. KP on, QP2 ; 9. KP : B,
Kt : P ; 10. KB QKt 3. Here Bertin (p. 6) makes Black
caftle ; and then, after 11. *QP*2, *KRP* 1, ftops fhort,
with the remark—" And the players may finifh the game,"
without expreffing any opinion which fhould win. In
another place, however, he makes a general remark, from
which we can fee, that he, as Philidor did after him,
confiders Black to have the beft of it ; to the tenth, namely, of his Rules (p. vi) he adds thefe words : " But the
defence, if well played, is ftill the beft againft the gambits, in which you change all your pieces, except the
gambit that gives three pawns, [in] which [it] will be
neceffary to keep a rook, to conduct your pawns to the
queen."

Philidor continues the game thus : QB K3 ; (*Second*

Variation) 11. QP 2, KKt K5. This Variation is furnifhed by him in order to juftify the cenfure, which he
had pronounced on QP2 as the eleventh move of White,
namely, that by fo playing (inftead of *QP*1) White would
make an opening for Black's Knights, and thus fpeedily
lofe the game. It will be feen, however, that precifely
in confequence of the entry of Black's Knight into White's
game, (by KKt K5,) and by the confequent move of the
King's Bifhop's Pawn (KBP2) to fupport the Knight
there, Black expofes himfelf, in Philidor's own continua-
tion of the game, to very ferious attacks.   12. QB KB4,
KBP2; 13. QKt Q2, Q K2; 14. QBP2, QBP1; 15. P :
P, P : P; 16. QR QB, QKt B3; 17. Kt : Kt, KBP : Kt;
18. Kt : Gambit P. (Here, by the way, Cozio [1766,
vol. ii. p. 375] more correctly plays *Kt K5*, with the
advantage on White's fide.)   Caftles KR; 19. Q Q2,
KRP1. Another very queftionable move. White would
win, were he to take advantage of it by making the attack
given in Bilguer's *Handbuch*, viz., 20. *QB : KRP.*   But
Philidor proceeds: 20. QR QB5, QR Q; 21. KB QR4,
KKtP2; 22. QB K3, R : R†; 23. Kt : R, Q Q3; 24.
Q KR2, K Kt2; 25. Q : Q, R : Q; 26. QRP1, K Kt3;
27. QKtP2, KRP1; 28. QKtP on, Kt K2; 29. R QB7,
R Q2; which brings us to the pofition, from which we
fet out.

II.

PHILIDOR AS CHESS-PLAYER.

AVING thus examined the *Analyſe*, in reference to its value as a work of Cheſs-
theory, it now remains to infer from it,
what was Philidor's ſtrength in actual play.
Such inferences, it muſt be owned, are by
no means certain, inaſmuch as authors rarely appear ſo
ſtrong in their works, as in games played over the board.
In the preſent caſe, however, it can be aſſerted with confidence, that, in ſpite of ſeveral inaccuracies in the *Analyſe*, we derive from it a higher opinion of Philidor's
ſtrength in play, than from the games, (of which we
have a conſiderable number,) which he played blindfold,
or over the board at odds. Nearly all of the genuine
games, that have been preſerved to us of Philidor and
other players of his day, were publiſhed by Mr. George
Walker, in 1835, in a ſmall volume, under the title of
*A Selection of Games at Cheſs played by Philidor and his
Contemporaries.* This author, who has enriched ſo many
departments of Cheſs-literature by his valuable contri-
butions, was enabled to throw ſome light upon the Phi-
lidorian Age, by becoming the fortunate purchaſer of the
Rev. George Atwood's Cheſs MSS., when the library of
that celebrated mathematician was expoſed to ſale by
auction. Mr. Atwood was known to have been among
the admirers and aſſociates of Philidor, and to have been
himſelf, moreover, no mean Cheſs-player. His MSS.

proved to be his own record of many games, played, between 1780 and 1800, by Count Brühl, Mr. Wilſon, Dr. Bowdler, Lord Harrowby, the Hon. Mr. Conway, Mr. Cotter, and Mr. Leyceſter, with De Beaurevoir, Philidor, Verdoni, and Mr. Atwood himſelf. Theſe ſpecimens are highly intereſting to the ſtudious inquirer; but—to ſpeak quite frankly—they give no very high idea of the Cheſs-ſkill of that day. Philidor, at any rate, was then in the evening of his life. In theſe games, the Old Maſter does indeed ſtand, under the keen inſpeƈtion of our eyes, far higher than his fellows; but he is by no means ſecure againſt committing, now and then, a ſtriking overſight. To explain how this ſhould happen, one or two circumſtances muſt be taken into conſideration. Philidor had, at that time, croſſed the boundary of threeſcore, and had, therefore, moſt certainly, long ſince left behind him the period of his greateſt ſtrength as a player,—a period, which cannot be conſidered as extending, upon an average, beyond the fortieth year of life. Nay, I am diſpoſed to believe, that the limit of the moſt perfeƈt correƈtneſs in play is, in very many caſes, reached conſiderably earlier: the long-continued occupation with the buſineſs of life aƈts, with weakening effeƈt, upon the power of *attention*, ſo eſſentially requiſite in Cheſs.

The ſecond conſideration, that operates to mitigate the ſeverity of our judgment, reſts upon the faƈt, that Philidor's adverſaries were players of only moderate ſtrength. Their weak and inaccurate ſtyle of play could not remain without its effeƈt upon him. For it is a truth, well eſtabliſhed by experience, that ſtrong players, when engaged with weak ones, can exert themfelves only fo far as to make fure of victory in a majority of games. The intenfity, with which they exert their faculty of combination, is at firft relaxed by careleffnefs, and afterwards by a haftinefs, that has become a habit. To play, moreover, giving heavy odds, although it may compel the ftronger player to exert his attention, does, neverthelefs, affect him injurioufly, upon the whole; becaufe, in fuch games, he calculates of courfe, and may calculate too much, upon the overfights of his adverfary.

If, under thefe complicated relations of the queftion, it is difficult to form a juft eftimate of Philidor's real ftrength, in comparifon with that of his contemporaries, it cannot but be doubly difficult to bring an earlier age into comparifon with a later one—efpecially when the later age is characterized by its remarkable advancement in Chefs-fcience—and to determine how Philidor would rank among the players of the prefent day. The opinion, which I have, neverthelefs, formed, is, that Philidor, when in the fulnefs and frefhnefs of his ftrength, with the folid fupport of his talent for analyfis, muft have poffeffed the capacity to make his own any given meafure of practical fkill; but that his Chefs-faculty had, by no means, attained, among fuch contemporaries, its higheft poffible degree of development; and that he, therefore, falls fomewhat fhort of that accuracy of conception and that richnefs of combination, which we behold with wonder in the victorious conteft of La Bourdonnais againft the united book-knowledge and genius of M'Donnell.

The judgment, which I have thus pronounced upon

Philidor and his Age, to many may appear to be unjuft. To give the reader an opportunity, therefore, to judge of its fairnefs and its foundnefs, I fhall proceed to lay before him a few games from Mr. Walker's publication, with the accompaniment of fome notes of my own. Before doing fo, however, I muft devote a few words to Philidor's playing without fight of board and men, or "blind-fold playing" (fo called.) Nine fuch games of his—each *triad* whereof was played fimultaneoufly—are familiar to all Englifh-reading Chefs-ftudents, inafmuch as they are contained in every current edition of PHILIDOR *on Chefs*. They firft appeared in the new edition of the *Analyfe*, which was publifhed in the Englifh language, at London, in 1790. This edition, which—if it had been really pre-pared by Philidor, as it bears his name, would be the third edition—exhibits indications, in the Preface and elfewhere, by which we recognife the faft, that it was merely fuperintended by the Publifher in the Author's name. The games in queftion belong to the years 1783, 1788, and 1790—to Philidor's old age, therefore; but even had they been the fruit of an earlier period, they could furnifh no criterion of his ordinary play. Their fpecial intereft confifts in the evidence, which they fur-nifh, of Philidor's rare gift of imaginative prefentation,— the power of keeping boards and men clearly before his "mind's eye,"—a gift that may be compared to the pe-culiar talent of thofe mental arithmeticians, who aftound us by the portentous computations, which they carry on in their head alone. It is worthy of remark, that Phili-dor fhould have retained this gift to the day of his death.

He never exhibited it, however—fo far as the number of his fimultaneous games is concerned—in the fulleft extent, to which it has been cultivated. Greater feats, of this kind, had been performed before his time ; greater feats have alfo been performed in our own day, when Mr. Louis Paulfen plays blindfold *ten* games at once.* Among the Afiatics, during the middle Ages, blindfold playing was fo much a favourite mode of play, that the Oriental Chefs-authors give fpecial inftructions for it. In this way we learn the fact, that Afiatic amateurs, who could conduct three or four blindfold games at once, and at the fame time recite verfes, were by no means rare. Nay, there is alfo faid to have been one player, in the Eaft, who had gone to the extent of playing fo many as ten fuch games at once.† Thefe examples go far beyond what Philidor's art ever achieved. Several games in Walker's *Selection* fhow, that Philidor, blindfold, played even with antagonifts, to whom, over the board, he was accuftomed to give the Queen's Knight for the King's Bifhop's Pawn and the move. And, upon the whole, it is reckoned, that Philidor, in blindfold play, was about a Pawn under his ufual ftrength.

To proceed with the games from Walker's *Selection*. In 1788, Philidor gives the Pawn and two moves to M.

---

* In a letter, written fome time after the date of the Effay, the author expreffes his regret, that no account of Paul Morphy's blindfold playing, at Birmingham and in the *Café de la Régence*, had reached him, in feafon to enable him to place the name of the young American mafter by the fide of Mr. Paulfen's.—Tr.

† Bland's *Perfian Chefs*, p. 24.

de Beaurevoir. This gentleman, being at that time (according to Mr. Walker) a Chefs-player of high ftanding in France, had expeƈted to be able to make a ftand againft Philidor at the Pawn and *one* move. He was beaten, notwithftanding, at the larger odds. Although the games of this match are by no means free from errors, they exhibit, in many places, a mafterly judgment of pofition, on the part of Philidor. It muft alfo be obferved, that his adverfary was not remarkably ftrong. He not only allowed himfelf to be vifibly frightened by Philidor's play—as often happens to the weaker party in fuch a match—but in faƈt he really poffeffed hardly fuch a meafure of talent, as would conftitute him, at the prefent day, what is called a "fecond-rate" player—fuch a player as ufually wins not more than one even game out of five from a mafter in Chefs.

FIRST GAME. (Remove Black's KBP from the board.) 1. (M. de Beaurevoir) KP2; 2. QP2, (Philidor) KP1; 3. KBP2. (KBP2 is no longer recommended at the prefent day; but formerly it was the ufual move. I do not, therefore, condemn it as weak play on the part of Beaurevoir.) QP2; 4. KP on, QBP2; 5. QBP1, QKt B3; 6. KKt B3, Q QKt3; 7. QRP1, QRP2; 8. QRP on. (The two laft moves of White fhow that he had as yet formed no plan how to ufe his Pieces for an attack— a proof either of embarraffment through fear, or of natural want of energy.) KKt R3; 9. KB Q3, QB Q2; 10. QKt R3, Caftles; 11. QKt Kt5, KKt B2; 12. QB K3, QBP on; 13. KB QB2. (This retreat of the Bifhop is difadvantageous. It would do better to go to *K2*, in

order to maintain the attack on Black's QB P. If Philidor fhould, thereupon, make the fame move as he does
in the actual game, White would get a very good attack:
e. g., 13. *KB K2, QKt Kt;* 14. *QKtP* 1, *QB : Kt;* 15.
P : B, Q : P; 16. *KKt Q2,* or *QKtP : P, QP : P;* 17.
QR R4, Q QKt 7; 18. *QB* home, *Q : QBP†;* 19. *B*
covers, *Q QKt7;* 20. *KB : P,* with a decifive attack.)
QKt Kt; 14. QKt R3, Q : QKtP. (White would have
done better to play 14. *Caftles, B : Kt;* 15. *P : B, Q:P;*
16. *Q Q2.*) 15. Kt QKt 5. (Here White facrifices a
Pawn, *poffibly* for the purpofe of getting room for his
attack, but *probably* becaufe he failed to fee, that 15. *Q*
QB would make his game fafe at every point: Black
could not then take *QBP* without lofing his Queen.)
B : Kt; 16. P : B, Q : QKtP; 17. KB QR4, Q QR3.
(In hopes of getting a chance to play *QKtP2,* which
would clear a fpace for defenfive purpofes. But the
combination does not fucceed. The Queen might have
alfo drawn back to *QKt3;* but fhe could not have gone
afterwards to *QB2:* the defence of *QKtP* would then
have been too difficult.) 18. QR QKt, KB K2; 19.
Caftles, Q QR2 (a *coup de repos;*) 20. Q QB2, KKtP1;
21. R QKt5. (A fingularly unfkilful move. Black takes
advantage of it immediately, to provide the neceffary
protection for his *QKtP.*) R Q2; 22. KR QKt, KKt
Q; 23. R QKt6, KKt QB 3; 24. KKtP2, KR KB; 25.
KRP2, R QB2; 26. K Kt2. (A blunder. White now
had a chance to call back his Rook from the idle adventure on which it had gone to *QKt6,* and fo prevent its
being cut off by *Kt QKt5.* After doing this, he might

have attempted, with the help of a Rook, to make a breach in Black's line of defence on the King's fide. The Black Queen is ftill in an unfavourable pofition, and could not readily come to the refcue of the other wing.) Kt QKt5 ; 27. QR : Kt, P : R ; 28. P : P, QKtP2. (Black lofes no time to fecure greater freedom of movement.) 29. KB : P, R QKt2 ; 30. KB : P. (White could have drawn his Bifhop back, with the lofs of a Pawn, to QR4. The facrifice of 30. *B : P* is, perhaps, founded on a bold, but unfound, combination, which— even if it could have been completely carried out—would not have been decifive for White, viz.: 30. *B : P, P : B;* 31. *Q : P†, K Q2;* 32. *QP* on, *Q : B;* 33. *P : P†, K* home; 34. *Q B8†, B* covers, &c.) R QB2 ; 31. Kt Q2, P : B ; 32. Kt : P, Q QKt2† ; 33. K Kt 3, QKt R3 ; 34. QK2, Kt : P. (Black could alfo have firft played 33. *Q Kt4;* and then, upon 34. *R QB, Kt QR3;* [35. *QK2, K Kt;*] 35. *QP* on, and *then B : P.*) 35. Kt Q6†, B : Kt ; 36. P : B, R QB6 ; 37. K R2, R QB7 ; 38. QB Q2, KR : P. (Black's laft move was a blunder—fuch a blunder as fhould never be made by a Mafter in Chefs. *KR : P* gives White a chance poffibly to draw the game ; whereas *K Q2* would have been a winning move. But White, as we fhall fee, does not avail himfelf of the chance thus given him. He replies with 39. *Q : P†,* without duly weighing all the confequences of the move. His attention may have been directed exclufively to the following combination : 39. *R : Kt, Q : R ;* 40. *Q : KP†, K QKt2;* [41. *Q K7†, K QR3 ;* 42. *Q K2†, Q* covers, or *K Kt3,* &c.] 41. *Q Q7†, K QR3 ;* 42. *K Kt3, Q : QP ;*

43. *B : R, Q Q6†,* &c.) 39. Q : P†, K Q. (If Black had
moved inſtead to Q Kt, he would juſt as little have
cut off White's chance to draw, as may be ſeen by the
following moves : 40. *Q K*8†, [*R QB ;* 41. *B : KR,*] *K
QR*7 ; 41. Q QR4†, Q covers ; 42. *Q Q*7†, *K* to corner ;
43. *Q K*8†, *R* covers ; 44. *P Q*7, &c.) 40. Q KKt8†,
K Q2 ; 41. Q : P†, K B. (White could now draw by
perpetual check.) 42. Q : Q†, K : Q ; 43. R : Kt†, K
B3 ; 44. K attacks R, KR KB8 ; 45. P Q5†, K : firſt P.
(Beaurevoir appears not to have been well ſkilled in end-
games ; otherwiſe, he would have played *B K*3, or ſtill
better *B KB*4, becauſe the Biſhop, beſides protecting the
Pawn, is alſo for the moment protected by the King.)
46. R Q4, K K4 ; 47. R Q3, K attacks R ; 48. R K3†,
K : P ; 49. R Q3†. (White acts evidently upon the erroneous impreſſion, that he is obliged to keep the Biſhop
at Q2.) K K5 ; 50. R K3†, K Q5 ; 51. R K2, K attacks
R ; 52. R attacks P, K : B ; 53. R : P, QR B6† ; 54. K
attacks R, KR B6 ; 55. KRP on, QR K6 ; 56. KRP on,
K K7 and wins.

SECOND GAME. (Remove Black's KBP from the board.)
1. (M. de Beaurevoir) QP2 ; 2. QBP2, (Philidor) KP1 ;
3. KP2, KKtP1 ; 4. KBP2. (I make no ſort of remark upon theſe introductory moves, becauſe ſkill in the
openings depends upon ſtudy ; and this branch of Cheſs-
ſtudy is far more advanced now, than it was in the time
of Philidor. I reſerve all criticiſm for the game proper.)
QP2 ; 5. QBP : P, KP : P ; 6. KP on, QBP2 ; 7. KB Q
Kt5†, QKt B3 ; 8. QKt B3, QRP1 ; 9. B : Kt†, P : B ;
10. QB K3, P : P ; 11. Q : P, KKt R3 ; 12. Q QKt6.

(In games at odds, the fecond player has ufually a bad
pofition, and is glad to bring about an exchange of Queens.
Here it is White that offers the exchange. The pofition
has, however, by this time become about equal, and I
will not, therefore, condemn Q QKt6 as a fin againft a
general principle. The move is, neverthelefs, to be
blamed, becaufe it muft bring White into a bad pofition,
or caufe him the lofs of a Pawn.) Q : Q ; 13. B : Q, QR
attacks B ; 14. QKt R4, KB QKt5† ; 15. K K2, Caftles ;
16. QRP1, KB K2 ; 17. KKtP1, QBP on ; 18. QR QKt,
(a perfeétly ufelefs move,) QB attacks R ; 19. QR Q,
QB K5 ; 20. KKt B3, QB QB7. (The Bifhop might
have gone at once to *QB7*. In that cafe, White's *KKt*
would have kept his place. Beaurevoir was, I fufpeét, a
player, to whom Philidor could have given the Knight :
the Mafter, therefore, plays careleflly.) 21. QB : P, B :
R† ; 22. R : B, B : B ; 23. Kt : B, R : P† ; 24. K B, Kt
KB4 ; 25. R Q3, KR QB ; 26. Kt QKt3, KR QB7 ; 27.
QKt Q2, QP on ; 28. K K2, QR QR7 ; 29. Kt : P.
(White fhould have prepared this move by *KKt P* on.
Philidor, however, did not take advantage of the blunder,
which ought (as Walker remarks) to have coft White the
lofs of a Piece.) Kt : Kt. (*R : Kt*† would have been the
better move. Both this game and that which follows
it exhibit fuch ferious blemifhes that I fhould not afcribe
them to Philidor, if there were the flighteft reafon to
doubt the genuinenefs of the Atwood MSS., which
Walker made ufe of for his *Seleétion*.—I may take this
occafion alfo to guard myfelf againft the fufpicion of having, on purpofe, chofen defeétive games, in order to make

out my cafe : the games, which I am now annotating,
are taken precifely as they come—the three firſt—in
Walker's book.) 30. R : Kt, R : P ; 31. KtP on, QR
KR6 ; 32. KBP on, R : P† ; 33. K Q, KR : Kt† ; 34.
R : R, R : R† ; 35. K : R, P : P ; 36. P : P, KRP2 ; 37.
KP on, QRP on and wins.

THIRD GAME. (Remove Black's KBP from the board.)
1. (M. de Beaurevoir) KP2 ; 2. QP2, (Philidor) KP1 ;
3. QBP2, KKtP1 ; 4. KBP2, QP2 ; 5. QBP : P, P : P ;
6. KP on, QBP2 ; 7. KB·QKt5†, QKt B3. (Thus far
this game is quite like the ſecond ; only that a move or
two are tranſpoſed. The players appear, therefore, to
have had a good memory for the mode, in which they
had played before. The two firſt games were played at
the ſame fitting, on the 31ſt of May, 1788. The third
followed in April.) 8. KKt B3, Q QKt3 ; 9. QKt B3,
P : P ; 10. KKt : P, KB pins Kt ; 11. QB K3, KKt K2 ;
12. QRP1, KB QB4.

(Walker, who accompanies the games with only here
and there a note, ſays here, that (Black) 12. *KB : QKt†*
would *apparently* have been better. It is clear, therefore, that he perceived, as little as Beaurevoir, (who continued with 13. QKtP2,) the groſs blunder, which Black
had fallen into—a blunder, which ſhould have coſt him
a Piece. The overſight is all the more ſtriking, that the
Biſhop—if it had been well for him to ſtand at QB4—
could have gone thither two moves earlier, inſtead of
going to QKt5. At that moment, *KB QB4* could have
been made without diſadvantage. The conſequences
would have been ſomewhat as follows :—11. *QKt QR4,*

*Q QR*4†; 12. QB covers, *KB QKt*5; 13. *QKt B*3, *KKt
K*2; 14. *Caſtles.* The following Variation ſhows the
neceſſary conſequences of the moves actually made:—
13. *QKt QR*4, *Q* checks; 14. *QKtP* covers, *KB : P*†;
15. *QRP : B, Q : P*†; 16. *K B*2. There is no ſtrength
in Black's paſſed Pawns. The poſition of his Queen is
bad likewiſe. Beſides, White can force an exchange of
Queens, if he likes. In an ancient Perſian MS., preſented by Major Yule to the Britiſh Muſeum, (No. 151,)
and deſcribed by Bland, (pp..18–25,) we find it related,
that " in India there was a player, who, during forty
years, never had a Pawn taken from him gratis." The
Perſian author adds, " *We* have never beheld ſucceſs like
this." That ancient Indian Cheſs-player muſt have poſ-
ſeſſed the power of attention in a far higher degree than
Philidor in 1788.)

The Game proceeds—13. QKtP2, B : Kt; 14. B : B,
Q QB2; 15. QB QB5, QB K3; 16. QB : Kt, Q : B; 17.
Kt : P, Q Q (Black's game is deſperate;) 18. Kt KB6†,
K B2; 19. Q KB3, Q QKt3; 20. B : Kt, P : B; 21. Kt
K4, B pins Kt; 22. Kt Q6†, K Kt2; 23. Q KB2, KR
KB; 24. KR B, QR Q (in hopes, evidently, to get ſome
chance to take off the Knight, who was ſteadily main-
taining his poſition;) 25. Q : Q, P : Q; 26. KKtP1,
KRP2; 27. KRP2, (a move by no means unwelcome to
Black, inaſmuch as it takes from the ſtrength of the White
Pawns, and gives greater ſecurity to the connexion be-
tween Black's Biſhop and his Pawns.) QKtP on, (thus
getting all his Pawns on white ſquares.) 28. K B2, R :
Kt. (Walker remarks on this move, which Black had

been for a long time getting ready to make, that "the facrifice was uncalled for." But upon this move hung Black's laft hope of poffibly drawing the game ; becaufe by getting the troublefome Knight out of the way, the Bifhop gains in ftrength. Although Philidor did not fucceed, even by this move, in extricating himfelf entirely from his difficulties, he neverthelefs proved himfelf to have been a far abler judge of the pofition, than the Editor of his games.) 29. P : R, KR Q; 30. KR K, R : QP; 31. KR K5, B K3; (becaufe, pofted here, the Bifhop clofes up the game, commands the fquares at KB4 and KKt5, and releafes the Rook, which otherwife was threatened with being fhut up by *QR Q.*) 32. QR K, K B3.

Walker remarks that the game was drawn, but that " the remainder was, unfortunately, not taken down." Beaurevoir (he adds) "could only have allowed his adverfary to draw the game through fome important mifcalculation," inafmuch as he had " a decided advantage." From thefe words it is clear, that Walker did not entirely underftand the nature of this end-game. Beaurevoir cannot have played *R : B†*, or this very elegant and decifive move (which evidently was not thought of by Walker) would have been noted down and preferved with the reft. White failed of winning the game, I fufpect, becaufe he was not fully aware of the Bifhop's ftrength for defence, and therefore did not take him off at all, or took him off in a lefs favourable pofition than the prefent. The confequences of taking him off at this moment would have been as follows :—1. *R : B†, R : R;* 2. *R : R†, K : R;* 3. *K B3, K B4;* 4. *KtP†, P : P†;* 5.

K Kt3, K K3; 6. *K : P, K B3*; 7. *KBP* on, *P : P†*; 8. *KB4* and wins, becaufe, while the Black King is taking *KRP*, the White King will be moving over to the other fide of the board, and the Black King will be too far behind him to be able to protect his Pawns at *QB3* and *QKt4*. There are other Variations, (as *e. g.* where the Black King goes over at once to the Queen's fide,) but by all of them Black muft lofe.

It would lead me too far, were I to prefent more games accompanied with full notes. Suffice it to repeat, that all of thefe games of Philidor's old age, taken from the Atwood MSS., contain fuch overfights as, under other circumftances, would rarely occur between good players. The games, moreover, taken all together—even when no odds are given (as in many of the blindfold-games)—are played entirely in the fpirit of that Chefs-period—that is to fay, with that want of elegance and brilliancy—nay, with that *clumfinefs*—in planning the combinations, which then prevailed throughout the North of Europe.

During Philidor's laft days, immediately preceding his death, his ftrength in play muft have fallen off confiderably, for he gave lighter odds. Atwood had been accuftomed to take the Queen's Knight, or the Queen's Rook, for the King's Bifhop's Pawn—on one occafion, for the Queen's Bifhop's Pawn. He appears, however, as the winner, in the majority of thofe games of Walker's *Selection*, that belong to the fummer of 1795. And the change certainly was not on Atwood's fide. He did not play particularly well—as may be feen by the following opening moves of a game, which bears date the 24th of

June, 1795, precifely two months, therefore, before Philidor's death :—(Philidor gives QR for KBP, and has
the move)—1. KP2, KP1 ; 2. QP2, QP2 ; 3. KP on,
QBP2 ; 4. QBP1, P : P ; 5. P : P, KB† ; 6. K K2, QKt
P1 ; 7. Q QR4†, QKt Q2 ; 8. Q : B, B QR3† ; 9. K K,
B : B ; 10. K : B, QR QB ; 11. QKt B3, Q KR5 ; &c.
The game has become reafonably equal, confidering that
the firft player had given the Rook ; but Philidor loft it,
at laft, for no other reafon, than becaufe he failed to
feize the initiative in the later combinations.   On the
28th and 29th of June, he gave Atwood only the Pawn
and Two Moves, in games, which were perhaps the
laft he ever played : thefe games he won.   In January
1796, Verdoni gave the fame Odds with fuccefs to Atwood, after having failed in the attempt to give him the
Knight.   It would appear from this, that Verdoni—
whom Sarratt, from perfonal acquaintance, defignates, in
his Treatife, (1808, p. xxii.,) as " inconteftably a player
of the firft order"—may probably have favoured Atwood.
If fuch were not the cafe, then we might agree with
Walker (1835, p. 74) in his inference, that " while the
games of Verdoni evince unqueftionable talents for invention, they prove the immeafurable fuperiority of Philidor."   Verdoni died at London about the year 1804.
As to what his real ftrength was, in comparifon with that
of Philidor, we happen to poffefs precife information.
We learn, namely, from a letter of Defchapelles to the
late celebrated Aftronomer, Schumacher of Altona, (printed in the *Berliner Schachzeitung* for 1848, pp. 274 and
327,) that Philidor did indeed give Verdoni the Pawn,

but that he referved to himfelf the Move. The difference of ftrength thus indicated was fo flight, that in our
day no attempt would be made to equalize it by any kind
of Odds.

But Walker does not ftop with inferring the inferiority
of Verdoni to Philidor: he croffes the boundary of the
eighteenth century, and, by affuming that Sarratt was ex-
actly equal to Verdoni, eftablifhes a means of comparifon
between the earlier and the later age, and comes to the
conclufion, that Philidor would have proved decidedly
fuperior to the Chefs-mafters of the prefent day. But
this comparifon refts on too uncertain a foundation. For,
in the firft place, as to the real ftrength of Verdoni, Sarratt may have rated it too high;—fince in his Treatife
(1808, p. 6,) he intimates, that his relations to Verdoni
were thofe of a mere beginner to an adept.* Under fuch
circumftances, the experienced player might well appear
to him to be greater than he really was. In the next
place, there is abfolutely nothing to go upon to prove
that Sarratt ftood upon the fame level with Verdoni. I
think myfelf authorized to fay, that the affumption of
fuch equality is certainly erroneous. The later generation of Chefs-players has not, indeed, fhewn itfelf particularly grateful for the hafty labours of Sarratt as a Chefs-

---

* From a letter of Mr. Lewis's to me, (as well as from Walker,
Selections, p. 61, *note,*) it appears that Sarratt ftood to Verdoni in the
relation of a *Pupil* to a *Teacher:* "Verdoni" (he fays) "was Sarratt's
mafter, and was fcarcely, if at all, inferior to Philidor, although he
learned the game in middle age."—TR.

author, although he really did good fervice, between the publication of his *Treatife* in 1808 and his death in 1821, both by his own works and by his abridged tranflations of the old Mafters; but even lefs juftice appears to have been meted out to him as a Chefs-*player*. Lewis—who in April 1821 had played with Defchapelles and was acquainted with the other Mafters of that day—" afferts, without hefitation," of Sarratt, on the 30th of November, 1822, (in the Preface to his tranflation of Carrera,) " that he was the fineft and moft finifhed player he had ever feen, alike excellent in attack and defence."* According to this, the efforts of Sarratt in practical fkill could not for a moment be put on the fame level with the moderately well-played games of Verdoni in Walker's *Selection*. I abide, therefore, by the opinion, that the players of the fecond half of the laft century were inferior to the Chefs-mafters of the more recent period. There can be no doubt, that the modern habit of making Chefs a fubject of theoretical ftudy—whether by private reading, or by playing with fkilful book-players—has contributed not a little to fuch fuperiority of our age over

---

* Mr. Lewis ftill expreffes the fame opinion. I may without impropriety give his very words; for although they occur in a private letter, they are but the fpecification of the general ftatement made public in 1822. "If the perfection of Chefs-playing" (he writes) "confifts in making the beft moves with the greateft rapidity, La Bourdonnais approached perfection nearer than any player I have ever known. I fhould, however, have backed both Defchapelles and SAR-RATT (both flow players) againft him, thinking them a fhade better." (*Letter* to G. A., March 5th, 1860.)—TR.

the paſt. The arduous labours of the Cheſs-author—in which I may claim to have had my ſhare—find their reward in the aſſurance, that they have been ſuccefsful in attaining the objeĉt they aimed at,—to raiſe the ſtandard and the charaĉter of aĉtual play.

Another element, to aſſiſt in determining the ſtrength of Philidor, is furniſhed by a game, which was publiſhed by La Bourdonnais in the firſt volume of the *Palamède*, (1836,) p. 392. It was played by him againſt the "Amateurs," Carlier and Bernard. Deſchapelles knew them both, and ſays, that when playing ſingly with Philidor, they received from him the Pawn and Move; but that when they played againſt him conſulting, Philidor either loſt, at theſe odds, or ſucĉeeded with difficulty in drawing the game. The following game, which dates from the year 1780, muſt be the oldeſt recorded ſpecimen of a "Conſultation-game." Philidor gives KBP, and loſes by his own fault.—1. (Carlier and Bernard) KP2, (Philidor) KP1; 2. QP2, QP2; 3. P : P, P : P; 4. Q R5†, P covers; 5. Q K5†, Q covers; 6. QB KB4, QBP1; 7. KB K2, KB Kt2; 8. Q : Q†, Kt : Q; 9. KKt B3, Caſtles; 10. QB K5, QKt Q2; 11. Caſtles, QKt : B; 12. Kt : Kt. ("White retakes with the Knight," ſays the *Palamède*, "in order to enable KBP afterwards to ſupport the Knight." We ſhall, however, preſently ſee, that both parties, for ſeveral moves, failed in forming a correĉt judgment of the poſition, which really gave Black a chance to win back his Pawn. The queſtion, whether the Pawn would have been loſt juſt as well, if White had played 12. *P : P,* I do not pauſe to examine thoroughly : appa-

rently, the Pawn might in that cafe have been fafe.)
B : Kt ; 13. P : B, KR B5. (The Rook goes one fquare
too far : it fhould have ftopt at *B*4. In that cafe, White's
paffed Pawn would have been loft. For the game muft
then have proceeded thus : 14. *KBP*2, *KKtP* on ; 15.
P : P, R : BP, and KP cannot be faved. This combination was obferved, neither by the parties nor by the *Palamède*, which afcribes the lofs of the game by Philidor
to the faft, that Black, by 12. *B : Kt*, allowed White to
get a paffed Pawn.) 14. KB Q3, QB KB4 ; 15. B : B,
Kt : B. (Philidor's moves lead, in the fimpleft poffible
way, to his defeat. It is difficult to fee why he did not
contrive to adopt another line of play. He ftill had it
in his power to take off the paffed Pawn : *e. g.* 15. . . .
R : B ; 16. *KBP*2, *KKtP* on ; 17. *P : P, R : BP*. The
game might then have proceeded fomewhat as follows :
18. *R K, Kt Kt*3 ; 19. *KP* on, *R K*4 ; 20. *Kt Q*2, *QR K*,
and Black wins the Pawn without danger.) 16. KKtP1,
KR K5 ; 17. KBP2, KR K7 ; 18. QKt R3, Kt K6 ; 19.
KR B2, R : R ; 20. K : R, Kt KKt5† ; 21. K Kt2, QR Q ;
22. KRP1, Kt KR3 ; 23. KKtP on, QRP1 ; 24. QR Q,
Kt KB2 ; 25. KRP on, QBP on ; 26. QBP1, QKtP2 ; 27.
Kt QB2, QRP1 ; 28. Kt K3, QP on ; 29. P : P, P : P ;
30. Kt QB2, QP on ; 31. Kt K, QP on ; 32. Kt KB3
and wins. This game appears to me to be well calculated to confirm the opinion, which I have before expreffed, concerning the Chefs-fkill of Philidor and his
contemporaries.

I clofe this difcuffion, by paffing in review the fuccef-
fion of great players, who have figured during the lateft

period of Chefs-hiftory. The lift begins with M. de
Kermuy, Sire de Légal. He attained to a very advanced
old age—to nearly ninety years. He was the teacher of
Philidor; but it was fettled, by the match of 1755, that
the mafter was decidedly inferior to his pupil. Up to
the time of his death, however, Légal maintained his
rank as the fecond player of France. Philidor was the
firft up to 1795. Of the fame period, and affociated
with him, were the Syrian Stamma, the fo-called *Amateurs,* Léger, Carlier, and Bernard, and efpecially Verdoni. The contemporary Italians, Rio, Ponziani, and
Lolli did not come into contaĉt with the Chefs-mafters
of Paris and London. We know nothing of any Spanifh
players of that period. The annals of Chefs fay as little
of any contemporary German celebrities. Count Brühl,
to be fure, (1737–1809,) nephew of the Saxon Minifter,
fo celebrated in the time of Frederic the Great, a German, but refident in England for the greater part of his
life, is named among the beft of the Englifh players.
Like them, however, he was decidedly inferior to Philidor. The tranfition from the laft to the prefent century
is formed by Verdoni, Carlier, and Bernard. With thefe
players, whofe celebrity dated from the former period,
the earlieft heroes of this century, Sarratt and Defchapelles were acquainted. To the fame clafs we fhould,
perhaps, refer Hypolite du Bourblanc, who perifhed by
fhipwreck in 1813. Sarratt, who had been on terms of
"intimate and uninterrupted friendfhip" with him fince
1798, mentions, (1821, vol. i. p. 29,) that his "remarkable genius and *brilliancy* of attack" were faid to be re-

produced in the ftyle of "the celebrated *Guillaume le Prêton*" (meaning Defchapelles.) In Germany, Allgaier croffes the boundary-line of the two centuries. Next after him, about the year 1820, comes Mendheim, of Berlin. Neither of thefe eminent players ever meafured their ftrength with each other or with any of the foreign celebrities. Of Sarratt alfo no matches are known; and, in like manner, the firft of the Ruffian great names, Petroff, has never—from the year 1824 to the prefent moment—come into contaĉt with the Weft. It is only during the very laft years, that America has begun to be heard from in the world of Chefs.

In France, Le Breton Defchapelles ranked for a long time as the firft player. He diftinguifhed himfelf, in 1821, againft La Bourdonnais and Cochrane. During the fame year, he gave the odds of the Pawn and Move, in three games, to Mr. Lewis, but without fuccefs. Thefe three games were firft made public by Greenwood Walker, in 1836, from the original minutes of the Englifh player. Mr. Lewis, however, has informed me, very lately,* that in writing down the games from memory, he had, unfortunately, tranfpofed fome of the moves in one of them. It is from this game, that the Pofition is taken, which is difcuffed in the *Schachzeitung* for 1855, (p. 17.) It was expeĉted, that a fecond match would have been contefted between Lewis and Defchapelles, in 1836; but the negotiation was ultimately

---

* A part of the only day (March 8th, 1858) fpent by the author in London, on his way to Rio Janeiro, was devoted to paying a vifit to Mr. Lewis.—TR.

broken off. Since that time the death of the French
player has occurred, and the Englifh mafter has withdrawn entirely from the practice of the game. The two-
celebrated pupils of thefe great players refpectively—La
Bourdonnais, who was at the height of his fame in 1836,
and M'Donnell—were prematurely loft to Chefs, by
death, before their mafters. We retain at the prefent
moment, therefore, only one great living witnefs of the
period, that has juft paffed away.

The links, ftill untold, in the chain of my enumera-
tion, are the players of the two laft decades of years, of
whom fome are now dead, fome ftill on the ftage. Their
names are too well known to need recital by me.

APPENDIX.

CORRECTIONS AND ADDITIONS.

P. 4. Note *. See efpecially the article *Des Maîtrifes* in a recent work, *La Mufique à l'Eglife par M. J. d'Ortigue*. Paris 1861. "Elles [les Maîtrifes] les renvoyaient à l'abri du foyer domeftique . . . . pourvus d'une éducation le plus fouvent fupérieure à celle des populations au milieu defquelles ils vivaient, et qui leur permettait de trouver de fuffifants moyens d'exiftence dans l'exercice de quelque profeffion honorable." (P. 85.)

P. 12. *Philidor bimfelf was living abroad at the time.* So I inferred from Twifs's citation from the *Encyclopédie;* but he had left out the clofing words of the article, viz., *Il eft maintenant à Paris,* which, however, have the appearance of being added after the body of the article had been written.

P. 21. Philidor undoubtedly went with Lanza as a *Singer.* I find, in the *Mercure français* for May 1770, that he fung one of his own *Motetts* in a *Concert Spirituel* of that year.

P. 29. My friend, Mr. William R. Henry—whofe knowledge of problem-literature is abfolutely exhauftive—has pointed out to me an earlier *Spieffruthenfpiel*, than Don Pietro Petronio's, in Gianutio (1597) f. 48, Ottavo partito *futtiliffimo di dieci tratti.*

P. 36. Thefe important facts (unknown even to Twifs) are given by Gerber upon better authority than mere goffip and tradition: he found them in the *Almanachs* and other authentic printed documents of the day. This I learn from my friend Mr. Thayer, (now in Vienna,) who has had occafion to colleƈt and ufe the fame documents for the Life of Beethoven, to which he has already devoted fo many years of ftudy and preparation.—In eftimating Philidor's pecuniary refources, (p. 89,) I negleƈted to mention the faƈt, that—befides being a penfioner of Louis XV.—he was alfo *Maître de Chapelle* to the Duke of Deux Ponts, an appointment to which, undoubtedly, fome falary was attached. This faƈt alfo refts upon the fole authority of Gerber; but we have feen that he is careful to "fpeak by the card;" and he is fuftained (to fome extent) by Philidor's dedication of his *Tom Jones* to *S. A. S. Monfeigneur le Duc Régnant des Deux Ponts, Prince Palatin du Rhin, Duc de Bavière, &c., &c.*

P. 58. Note. The career of a grandfon of Philidor's—Alphonfe, a violinift and pupil of Baillot—is beautifully traced by M. Scudo, in the fecond volume of his *Critique et Littérature Muficales.*

Pp. 66–8. I have made fad work, in my text, with the relations of Philidor and Gluck, becaufe the authorities, on which I was forced to rely, were all bent on being wrong ƒn fome way: Fétis, in particular, who, in the fubftance of his defence, is certainly right, is inexcufably wrong in fome of the details.; and Sévelinges, who is effentially and wickedly wrong, in the gift and *animus* of his accufation, is, after all, right where Fétis is wrong. Now that I have the help of the original authority, Favart, I will try to put thefe matters to rights here.—A year *before* the reprefentation of Philidor's *Sorcier*—viz., early in 1763 —Gluck's friend, Count Durazzo, fent the fcore of the *Orfeo* to his correfpondent, Favart, to have it engraved in Paris. Favart applied to Duni to correƈt the proofs. This Duni pofitively refufed to do, on any terms; becaufe, on examining the "copy," he found it full of errors, which he would not take the refponfibility or the trouble of correƈting. At length, on the 19th of April, Favart writes to the Count:—"I have had the fcore fhown to Philidor, and he does not prove by any means fo hard to deal with as the reft. He offers to make the preliminary correƈtions of the fcore *gratis*, and to fuperintend the engraving in perfon. He afks nothing of your Excellency but a copy of the work. While reading the fcore, at feveral places, he was affeƈted to tears. He always held the talents of the Chevalier Gluck in high efteem; but now that he has come to know the *Orfeo*, his efteem has rifen to veneration." (*Mémoires*, t. ii. p. 102.)—André Philidor is, therefore, wrong: it was the engraving, and not the reprefentation, of the *Orfeo*, (before it became the *Orphée*,) which his father fuperintended. Sévelinges is wrong (and, judging by the fpirit of his article, calumnioufly wrong) in charging, that Philidor ftole from the *Orfeo*, note for note, the romance, *Objet de mon amour*. Fétis is right in refuting this charge of plagiarifm by appealing to an infpeétion of the two fcores, and thus demonftrating that the *corpus deliéti* was a nonentity; but he is wrong, in turn, when he fays, that Philidor could not have known the *Orfeo* in feafon to commit the theft. He is wrong, moreover, in faying, that Sévelinges charged Philidor with the plagiarifm on the authority of Favart: Sévelinges merely cites Favart to fhow, that Philidor had in his hands the fcore of the *Orfeo* while at work on his own *Sorcier*.* Fétis is alfo wrong, in fo far as he creates the impreffion, that Favart regarded Philidor as a plagiarift: Favart uniformly expreffes himfelf as the friend and admirer of Philidor. And, finally, Fétis is careleffly wrong in faying, (as he does, in his fecond edition,) that it was Duni who fuperintended the engraving of the *Orfeo*.

P. 70. Note. More than this—Mr. Fifke has fhown (*Chefs Monthly* for January 1861,) that Count Brühl went to Paris in September 1755, (a year after Philidor's return home,) and lived there, as an *attaché* of the Saxon embaffy, until March 1759. The "laft vifit" was probably that which he made (according to Mr. Fifke) in 1785.

P. 74. I have fortunately difinterred, from the *Mercure français* for Auguft 1771, the original Profpeétus of Philidor's Second Edition. Confidering the date, it becomes highly probable, that Philidor's trip

---

* Fétis would have done better fervice, if he had driven his ftake through Sévelinges, as a logical *felo de fe*: the fhortfighted *advocatus diaboli* proves, namely, that Philidor muft certainly have committed the alleged theft, by proving that Philidor had, fix months before, put it in the power of every mufician and mufical critic in Paris to make inftant deteétion and expofure of the theft.

to England in 1772 was made (under the encouragement of Count Brühl and other friends) for the fpecial purpofe of obtaining fubfcribers to his book, and that a part of the lift was formed before the Chefs-Club was organized, and the final arrangement made for his annual vifit.

P. 75. Note †. Of courfe, I bafed my argument upon the belief, that "notre milord Goy" was fairly equal to "our Englifh friend, Goy," who—being, in French parlance, a *milord anglais*—might be a Peer, and could not be lefs than a gentleman. I knew not whether to be more amazed or amufed, when I ftumbled upon the evidence, in Walckenaer's *Vie d'Horace*, (t. i. p. 383,) that "mylord Goy" was the *fobriquet* of a remarkable French *farceur*—an *obligato* appendage of the higheft Parifian fociety—of whom Favart (t. ii. p. 239) tells a ftrange anecdote. But fuch men take the beft care of themfelves—when they have money; and my argument may ftill, perhaps, be as found as ever.